Max Heindel's Letters to Students

By

Max Heindel

Published by Left of Brain Books

Copyright © 2023 Left of Brain Books

ISBN 978-1-396-32632-5

First Edition

All rights reserved. No part of this publication may be reproduced, distributed, or transmitted in any form or by any means, including photocopying, recording, or other electronic or mechanical methods, without the prior written permission of the publisher, except in the case of brief quotations permitted by copyright law. Left of Brain Books is a division of Left Of Brain Onboarding Pty Ltd.

PUBLISHER'S PREFACE

About the Book

For eight years Max Heindel, the mystic and occultist sent out to the students of The Rosicrucian Fellowship a letter each month filled with much valuable information, explaining the cause of many of the difficulties occurring in daily life, not only of individuals but of nations as well, and giving a feasible solution of them. These letters, ninety-seven in number, sent out between Christmas 1910 and January 1919, constitute the subject matter of this book.

About the Author

Max Heindel (1865 - 1919)

"Max Heindel - born Carl Louis von Grasshoff in Aarhus, Denmark on July 23, 1865 - was a Christian occultist, astrologer, and mystic. He died on January 6, 1919 at Oceanside, California, United States.

He was born of the royal family of Von Grasshoffs, who were connected with the German Court during the lifetime of Prince Bismark. The father of Max Heindel, Francois L. von Grasshoff, migrated, when quite a young man, to Copenhagen, Denmark, where he married a Danish woman of noble birth. They had two sons and one daughter. The oldest of these sons was Carl Louis Von Grasshoff, who later adopted the pen name of Max Heindel. The father died when the eldest son was six years of age, leaving the mother with her three small children in very straitened circumstances. His infancy was lived in genteel poverty. His mother's self-denial was carried to an extreme in order that the small income would suffice that her sons and daughter could have private tutors so that they might take their place in society as members of nobility.

At the age of sixteen years, refusing a foreseeable future among the nobility class, he left home to enter the ship-yards at Glasgow, Scotland in order to learn the engineering profession. He was soon chosen as Chief Engineer of a trading steamer, position which took him in trips all over the world and gave him a great deal of knowledge of the world and its people. For a number of years he was Chief Engineer on one of the large passenger steamers of the Cunard Line plying between America and Europe. From 1895 to 1901, he was an ill luck consulting engineer in New York City and during this time he married, the marriage being terminated by the death of his wife in 1905. A son and two daughters were born of this marriage.

In 1903, Max Heindel moved to Los Angeles, California, in order to look for a job. Meanwhile, due to his earlier years that had been full of sorrow and to sad events in his own life, an increasingly intense desire to understand the cause of the sorrows and sufferings of humanity began to grow within him, as well as a desire to help alleviate them. Giving a new course to his life, he became interested in the study of metaphysics and, after attending lectures by the theosophist C.W. Leadbeater, he joined the Theosophical Society of Los Angeles, of which he was vice-president in 1904 and 1905. He also became a vegetarian and began the study of astrology, which he found to his delight gave him the key by means of which he found he could unlock the mysteries of man's inner nature. At this time, he met Augusta Foss who was also interested along similar lines of research and in astrology; she would become his future wife. However, overwork and privation brought on him a severe heart trouble in 1905 and for months he lay at the point of death but upon recovery he was even more keenly awake to the needs of humanity. It is said that much of the time during this illness he spent out of the body, consciously working and seeking for the truth as he might find it on the invisible planes.

From 1906 to 1907 he started a lecture tour, in order to spread his occult knowledge, in San Francisco and then in Seattle and in the northern part of the country. After a course of lectures in that city he was again forced to spend some time in a hospital with valvular heart trouble. Still undaunted, he once more took up his work of lecturing in the northwestern part of the United States.

In the fall of 1907, during a most successful period of lectures in Minnesota, he travelled to Berlin (Germany) with his friend Dr. Alma Von Brandis, who had been for months trying to persuade him, in order to hear a cycle of lectures by a teacher in the occult field called Rudolf Steiner. During his stay at Germany, he developed a sincere admiration by the personality of this knowledgeable lecturer, as latter shown in a dedication of his magnum opus, but at the same time he understood that this teacher had little to give to him. It was then, with his mind already made up to return, feeling that in vain he had given up a big work in America to take this trip, that Heindel reports to have been visited by a Spiritual being (clothed in his vital body).

This highly evolved entity later identified himself as an Elder Brother of the Rosicrucian Order, an Order in the inner worlds formed in the year 1313 and having no direct connection to physical organizations which call themselves by this name. As he afterwards mentions, the Elder Brother gave him information which was concise and logical and beyond anything he was capable of writing. Later, he found out that during a previous visit of the Elder Brother, he was put to a test to determine his worthiness to be messenger of the Western Wisdom Teachings. He recounts that only then he was given instruction how to reach the etheric Temple of the Rose Cross, near the German/Bohemian border, and how at this Temple he was in direct communication with and under the personal instructions of the Elder Brothers of the Rose Cross. The Rosicrucian Order is described as being composed of twelve Elder Brothers, gathered around a thirteenth who is the invisible Head. These great Adepts, belonging to human evolution but having already advanced far beyond the cycle of rebirth, are reported as being among those exalted Beings who guide mankind's evolution, the Compassionate Ones.

Heindel returned to America in the summer of 1908 where he at once started to formulate the Rosicrucian teachings, the Western Wisdom Teachings, which he had received from the Elder Brothers, published as a book entitled The Rosicrucian Cosmo-Conception in 1909. It is a reference work in the Christian mysticism practice and in the Occult study literature, containing the fundamentals of Esoteric Christianity from a Rosicrucian perspective. The Cosmo contains a comprehensive outline of the evolutionary processes of man and the universe, correlating science with religion.

From 1909 to 1919, suffering a severe heart condition and with an adverse financial situation, but with an indomitable will and great energy, Max Heindel was able to accomplish the great work for the Brothers of the Rose Cross. With the help, support and inspiration of his wife Augusta Foss, to whom in August 1910 he was joined in marriage, he gave successful teaching lectures; he sent correspondence lessons to the students, who formed groups in many of the larger cities; he wrote volumes which are translated into many languages all over the world; he founded The Rosicrucian Fellowship in 1909/11 at Mount Ecclesia, Oceanside (California); he published the Christian Esoteric magazine Rays from the Rose Cross in 1913 and, above all, he launched the Fellowship's Spiritual Healing service.

It is described that, at his death, his body dropped slowly as if loving hands were holding him and laying him down gently; as he looked up, smiling into Mrs. Heindel face, he spoke his last words: "I am all right dear".

Last, it is worthy of mention that the work prepared by Max Heindel, has been, since then, continued through students of the Western Wisdom Teachings who, as Invisible Helpers of mankind, assist the Elder Brothers of the Rose Cross to perform the Spiritual Healing around the world. This is the special work in which the Rosicrucian Order is interested and is provided according to the commands of Christ, namely, "Preach the gospel and heal the sick.""

(Quote from wikipedia.org)

CONTENTS

PUBLISHER'S PREFACE
FOREWORD 1
   FRIENDSHIP AS AN IDEAL 2
   SOUL GROWTH THROUGH DOING 4
   UNSELFISH SERVICE TO OTHERS 5
   A PLEA FOR THE CHURCH 7
   VALUE OF RIGHT FEELING 8
   HEALING THE SICK.. 10
   BAPTISM OF WATER AND OF SPIRIT 13
   RULING OUR STARS.. 15
   INVISIBLE GUARDIANS OF HUMANITY 17
   FLESH FOOD AND ALCOHOL 19
   PREPARATIONS FOR REMOVAL TO MT. ECCLESIA 21
   GROUND-BREAKING FOR FIRST BUILDING ON 23
   GENERATIVE PURITY THE IDEAL FOR THE WEST............................. 25
   THE COMING AGE OF AIR 27
   THE ROLE OF STIMULANTS IN EVOLUTION 29
   NECESSITY FOR DEVOTION 31
   STRAGGLERS IN EVOLUTION 33
   KEYNOTE OF THE ROSICRUCIAN TEACHINGS 35
   SACREDNESS OF SPIRITUAL EXPERIENCES 37
   INITIATIVE AND PERSONAL FREEDOM 39
   THE CHRIST SPIRIT AND THE SPIRITUAL PANACEA 41
   THE MYSTIC BREAD AND WINE 43
   DESCENDING AND ASCENDING ARCS OF EVOLUTION 45
   THE ROSICRUCIAN FELLOWSHIP, AS SPIRITUAL CENTER 47
   THE MYSTIC MESSAGE OF CHRISTMAS 50
   SERVICE TO OTHERS DURING THE NEW YEAR 52
   SIEGFRIED, THE TRUTH SEEKER... 54
   THE INCORPORATION AND FUTURE PLANS OF THE FELLOWSHIP.................. 56
   FREE MASONRY, CO-MASONRY, AND CATHOLICISM 58
   THE ROLE OF EVIL IN THE WORLD 60
   CHRIST, AND HIS SECOND COMING 62
   THE VITAL BODY OF JESUS 64
   IMPROVING OUR OPPORTUNITIES 66
   A PLEA FOR PURITY 68
   THE FAUST MYTH AND THE MASONIC LEGEND............................... 70
   EASTERN AND WESTERN METHODS OF DEVELOPMENT 72
   THE REASON FOR THE MANY DIFFERENT CULTS 74

WHAT THE PUPIL MAY EXPECT OF THE TEACHER	76
WHERE SHALL WE SEEK TRUTH, AND HOW SHALL WE KNOW IT?	78
WHY THE TRUTH SEEKER MUST LIVE IN THE WORLD	80
A METHOD OF DISCERNING TRUTH FROM ITS IMITATION	82
OUR RESPONSIBILITY IN GIVING OUT TRUTH	84
WOMAN'S SUFFRAGE AND MORAL EQUALITY	86
THE VICE OF SELFISHNESS AND THE POWER OF LOVE	88
INITIATION NOT TO BE ATTAINED THROUGH BREATHING EXERCISES	90
THE WORLD WAR AND INFANT MORTALITY	92
THE INVISIBLE HELPERS AND THEIR WORK ON THE BATTLE FIELD	94
THE WORLD WAR AND UNIVERSAL BROTHERHOOD	96
DESIRE--A TWO-EDGED SWORD	98
SPIRITUAL PROSPERITY FOR THE NEW YEAR	100
LOVE, WISDOM, AND KNOWLEDGE	102
CONCENTRATION IN THE ROSICRUCIAN WORK	104
THE COSMIC MEANING OF EASTER	106
WASTE THROUGH SCATTERING ONE'S FORCES	108
EPIGENESIS AND FUTURE DESTINY	110
THE NEED OF SPREADING THE TEACHINGS	112
ASTROLOGY AS AN AID IN HEALING THE SICK	114
UNNATURAL MEANS OF ATTAINMENT	116
THE RACE SPIRITS AND THE NEW RACE	118
THE WAR AN OPERATION FOR SPIRITUAL CATARACT	120
CYCLIC MOVEMENTS OF THE SUN	122
THE TEACHER'S DEBT OF GRATITUDE	124
SPIRITUAL TEACHERS--TRUE AND FALSE	126
THE BATTLE THAT RAGES WITHIN	128
EASTER, A PROMISE OF NEWNESS OF LIFE	130
DAILY EXERCISE IN SOUL CULTURE	132
THE REAL HEROES OF THE WORLD	134
THE WORK OF THE RACE SPIRITS	136
STRUGGLES OF THE ASPIRING SOUL	137
BUILDING FOR THE FUTURE LIFE	139
DESCENT OF THE CHRIST LIFE IN THE FALL	141
THE REASON FOR THE TRIALS THAT BESET THE OCCULT STUDENT	143
SPIRITUAL STOCK-TAKING DURING THE HOLY SEASON	145
ALL OCCULT DEVELOPMENT BEGINS WITH THE VITAL BODY	147
SERVING WHERE BEST FITTED TO SERVE	149
"LOST SOULS" AND STRAGGLERS	151
THE UNNECESSARY FEAR OF DEATH	152
HEART DEVELOPMENT AND INITIATION	154
SACRIFICE AND SPIRITUAL PROGRESS	156
ADJUSTING THE TEACHINGS TO THE UNDERSTANDING OF OTHERS	158
THE VALUE OF REVIEWING PAST LESSONS	160
TAMING AN UNRULY MEMBER	161
AN INNER TRIBUNAL OF TRUTH	163

EPIGENESIS AND THE LAW OF CAUSATION 165
THE PRESENT SORROW AND THE COMING PEACE 167
GOD--THE SOURCE AND GOAL OF EXISTENCE 168
THE NECESSITY OF PUTTING TALENTS TO USE 170
THE NOBILITY OF ALL LABOR 172
THE AQUARIAN AGE AND THE NEW COVENANT 174
MEAT EATING AND FUR WEARING 176
TOLERANCE OF OTHERS' BELIEFS 178
THE PURPOSE OF WAR AND OUR ATTITUDE TOWARD IT 180
THE INNER POWER AND THE RESPONSIBILITY THAT GOES WITH IT 182
EQUIPOISE OF GREAT HELP IN TIMES OF STRESS 184
THE OPTIMISTIC ATTITUDE AND FAITH IN ULTIMATE GOOD 186
INCREASING THE LIFE OF THE ARCHETYPE 188
THE LAW OF SUCCESS IN SPIRITUAL MATTERS.. 190

FOREWORD

FOR eight years Max Heindel, the mystic and occultist sent out to the students of The Rosicrucian Fellowship a letter each month filled with much valuable information, explaining the cause of many of the difficulties occurring in daily life, not only of individuals but of nations as well, and giving a feasible solution of them. These letters, ninety-seven in number, sent out between Christmas 1910 and January 1919, constitute the subject matter of this book.

Being the authorized messenger of the Brothers of the Rosicrucian Order and consequently in close touch with them, Mr. Heindel was continuously receiving and giving out occult information to his students relative to the past, present, and future evolution of life and form, which on account of his tutelage under the Brothers of the Order he was able to verify for himself and to which he was able to add many details. The letters in this book give many side lights on the Rosicrucian philosophy and many practical, helpful hints for living the life of the Christian mystic.

In many of these letters there is a reference to accompanying lessons. Each letter was accompanied by a lesson in pamphlet form. The greater part of these lessons have already been published in book form, and are available for reference by readers of this book. The volumes of lessons published to date are as follows: FREEMASONRY AND CATHOLICISM; THE WEB OF DESTINY; MYSTERIES OF THE GREAT OPERAS; THE MYSTICAL INTERPRETATION OF CHRISTMAS; AND GLEAMINGS OF A MYSTIC. The lessons not already published will appear later in a second volume of GLEAMINGS OF A MYSTIC. The readers of these letters will obtain much more from them if they will consult the corresponding lessons as they proceed.

In giving these letters to the world we feel that we are making a contribution of permanent value and importance, and one from which the student of esotericism will obtain much assistance in his progress on the Path.

FRIENDSHIP AS AN IDEAL

IN a religious movement it is customary to address one another as "sister" and "brother," in recognition of the fact that we are all children of God, who is our common Father. Brothers and sisters are not harmonious at all times, however. Sometimes they are even misguided enough to hate one another, but between friends there can be no feeling but love.

It was a recognition of this fact which prompted the Christ, our great and glorious Ideal, to say to His disciples: "Henceforth I call you not servants. . . .but friends." (John 15:15) We cannot do better than follow our great Leader in this as in all other things. Let us, therefore, not merely be content with the fraternal relationship, but let us endeavor to be friends in the very holiest and most intimate sense of the word.

The Elder Brothers, whose beautiful teachings have brought us together upon the Way of Attainment, honor their disciples in the same way that Christ honored His apostles, namely, by giving them the name of "friend." If you persist in the way upon which you have started, you will sometime stand in their presence and hear that name utters in a voice so soft, so kind, and so gentle that it beggars description or even imagination. From that time there will be no task you would not perform to deserve that friendship. It will be your one wish, your one aspiration, to serve them, and no earthly distinction will appear worthy of comparison with that friendship.

Upon my unworthy shoulders has fallen the great privilege of transmitting the teachings of the Elder Brothers to the public in general and to the students, probationers, and disciples of the Rosicrucian Fellowship in particular. You have requested that your name be placed on my correspondence list, and I gladly extend to you the right hand of fellowship, greeting you by the name of FRIEND. I appreciate the trust you repose in me, and I assure you that I shall endeavor to aid you in every way within my power to deserve your trust. I hope that you will also aid me in my work for yourself and others by a charitable judgment of any shortcomings you may discover in me or in my writings. None need the prayers of others so much as one who must be a leader.

Please remember me in your devotions, and be assured that you shall have a place in mine.

I enclose the first lesson in the hope that the foregoing may establish our relations upon a footing of sincere friendship.

SOUL GROWTH THROUGH DOING

I hope that you thoroughly studied the Christmas lesson and are thoroughly familiar with the phenomenon of the spiritual ebb and flow in the universe so that you will be able to give a reason for your faith in "holy Night." In this month's lesson the idea is carried to a further conclusion, not previously taught publicly. There are other teachings in this little lesson which shed a clearer light upon the immaculate mystery-birth than has ever been given before, and I hope that you will diligently study it during the coming month so that you may realize to the full the transcendent beauty of the sublime Rosicrucian teaching on this subject.

But whether you have studied the Christmas lesson and are able to discourse upon the spiritual ebb and flow or whether you will be able to expound the Immaculate Conception at the end of this month is after all secondary in importance to what you answer to the following question: Did you take advantage of the flood tide of spirituality at Christmas to seek out some one in distress as suggested in the last paragraph of the lesson? Did you put it to practical use in the world's work? I hope you did, for only as we practice the teachings in our immediate circle of influence will they bear fruit in soul growth. We may read till we get mental indigestion, but actions speak louder than words. Also there is a bad place said to be paved with good intentions. Therefore, dear friend, let me urge upon you the necessity of doing! doing! doing! Often we see in the home, office, shop, or assembly room that a certain things ought to be done. But the attitude of the man of the world is to shirk. He turns away saying: Why should I do it? Let some one else attend to it. We should reason differently, however. We should not plan how little we can do. If so we are not fitting ourselves to become Invisible Helpers. If we see that a task has to be performed, we should say to ourselves: Some one will have to do that; WHY NOT I? In this coming month dear friend, let us take as a spiritual exercise the following of this motto, "Why not !?" If we follow it consistently, we shall reap a greater blessing than we confer upon others.

May God abundantly bless you and strengthen you in your efforts.

UNSELFISH SERVICE TO OTHERS

YOU have of course studied in some measure the various teachings of the Rosicrucian Order, and when I address myself to you, it is not as if I were speaking to a stranger who is unfamiliar with the teachings or perhaps even skeptical of the existence of such an Order. These teachings have spread like wildfire in the Western world during the past two years, and that of itself shows a power behind them which is not of the ordinary human kind. This you will probably realize better when you have read the lesson for this month, which deals with this mysterious Order and shows it relation to the Rosicrucian Fellowship.

Has it ever occured to you to inquire, my dear friend, what binds you to this Fellowship? You know there are not outward bonds, that you have taken no oath of allegiance, and that you have not been intrusted with any secrets. What then constitutes the Fellowship of which we speak? It cannot be the teachings, for they are open to the whole world and are assented to by many who have not requested that they be enrolled as students. Neither is it the enrollment as a student which creates the inner bond, for many study only to benefit THEMSELVES and have not fellowship with the rest of us. Rather, it is the SERVICE which we perform and the earnestness wherewith we practice the teachings and become living examples to the world of that brotherly love which Christ spoke of as fulfillment of all commandments.

Last month we took for our motto the thought that if a certain task were to be performed which seemingly belonged to no one in particular, we would say, "Why not I?" instead of letting some one else do it or letting it lie. I trust you have performed this unselfish service often, and thus cemented the bonds of fellowship.

In this coming month I would ask you to give your thoughts and your efforts to advance the teachings of the Fellowship. Do not attempt to convince any one against his will or to proselyte, but try to find out in an unostentatious manner what bothers your neighbor in a spiritual way. Then try to help him with our teachings. But whether you say anything to him about where you received them or not must depend upon your own judgment. The main thing is to spread the teachings, not to advertise the Rosicrucian Fellowship.

A PLEA FOR THE CHURCH

LAST month I promised to take up further elucidation of the Rosicrucian Order and its relation to the Fellowship, but I forgot that Easter was at hand and would require attention first. I hope you will agree that it is more important to study this great cosmic event, particularly as we live in a Christian land and, I hope, are Christians at heart. In fact, dear friend, the keynote of what I would bring out this month is really A PLEA FOR THE CHURCH, and it is with that end in view that I have printed the poem, "Creed or Christ?" at the end of the lesson.

We are all Christ in the making, the love nature is unfolding in us all, and why should we not identify ourselves with one or another of the Christian churches which cherish the Christ ideal? Some of the best workers in the Fellowship are members, yes, and ministers, of churches. Many are hungry for what we feed upon. WE cannot share it with them by standing aloof, and we do ourselves harm by neglecting to take advantage of the great opportunity to aid in elevating the church.

Of course there is no compulsion. You are not REQUIRED to join or attend a church, but if you do go there in the spirit of helpfulness, I can promise you that you will experience a most wonderful soul growth in a very short time. The great Recording Angels, who give to each nation the religion best suited to its needs, placed us in a Christian land, because the Christian religion will help us in soul growth. Even admitting that it has been obscured by creed and dogma, we should not let that prevent us from accepting those teachings which are good, for that would be as foolish as to center our attention upon the spots in the sun and refuse to see its glorious light.

Please think this matter over, dear friend, and let us take for our motto this month, GREATER USEFULNESS, that we may grow abundantly by striving to improve our opportunities.

VALUE OF RIGHT FEELING

I hope you enjoyed last month's lesson. Perhaps you will think it strange, but I have fairly reveled in it myself, for it aroused by devotion most powerfully to think how the Divine Life pours itself out for us periodically so that we may have more abundant life. Without that annual influx of God's life, all life, or rather form, would cease to exist. It is by FEELING the higher emotions that we raise ourselves the easiest. It is good to study and to develop our minds, but there is a great danger in this age of becoming ensnared in the meshes of intellect. Paul struck the nail on the head when he said: "Knowledge puffeth up, but love edifieth." We all wish to KNOW; it is natural that we should, but unless our knowledge serves to make us better men and women, better SERVANTS to our fellows, it does not make us GREATER in the sight of God. Therefore cultivation of RIGHT FEELING is of enormous importance, and I sincerely hope that you have FELT the Easter lesson for that is the only way to get full benefit from it.

Picture to yourself that great wave of divine energy projected from the Invisible Sun which is the manifestation of the Father. Try to feel the awe you would experience if you could see it, as the trained seer can and does. Watch it in imagination as it strikes the earth on Holy Night at Christmas. Let the feeling work upon you about the way it sinks into the earth and is the active cause of the germination in all kingdoms. Christ used the simile of the brooding hen to describe His feelings towards other beings, and if you try to FEEL the sprouting of all things in nature as indicated in our Easter lesson, you will realize a side of the subject which may have escaped you.

I hope that you will long use this lesson as material for mediation as it is different from one of the intellectual lessons that may be grasped by the mind and put aside. This lesson is of PERMANENT VALUE, and the oftener you take it up and let it work upon your heart. the more closely you will come to THE HEART OF THINGS, which is God, the great and loving Father who pours out His life alike for the tiniest plant and the tallest monarch of the forest; who cares for beast and bird, for the outcast and homeless rover, and for the royal potentate in his palace, without discrimination.

May God abundantly bless you and open up to you the storehouse of His riches, which surpass all earthly enjoyments, and may you FEEL the wave of love which He pours out afresh from year to year as a reality. Then you will never be lonely if you are alone, and you will be, oh! so much richer, no matter how much you are blessed with earthly love, and so much more able to radiate that most sublime of all emotions, Spiritual Love.

HEALING THE SICK

CHRIST gave two commands to His disciples when He said: "PREACH THE GOSPEL, AND HEAL THE SICK." We saw in last month's lesson how closely the office of spiritual advisor is linked with healing of physical ailments, for though the immediate and apparent cause of disease may be physical, in the final analysis all ailments are due to transgression of the LAWS OF GOD, which we usually call "LAWS OF NATURE" in our materialistic attempts to eliminate the Divine. Bacon, with rare spiritual perception, said: "God and Nature differ only as the seal and the imprint." As flexible sealing wax is molded to the rigid lines of the seal, so also nature passively conforms to the immutable laws of its Divine Creator, and thus health and a carefree condition are the rule among the lower kingdoms. But when the human stage is reached, when individuality is evolved and we begin to demand choice, prerogative, and emancipation, we are apt to transgress the laws of God, and suffering invariable follows.

There is a side of the moon which we never see, but we know it is there, and that hidden side of the moon is just as much a factor in creating the tides as the part of the moon which is nearest to us and visible. So there is also a hidden side to man which is as productive of action as the physical being we behold. Transgressions of divine laws upon the mental and moral planes of action are quite as responsible for physical disorders as the hidden side of the moon is effective in producing the tides.

If the above were understood, physicians would no longer puzzle over the annoying fact that while a certain kind and quantity of medicine produces a cure in one cause, it may be absolutely impotent in others. A large and increasing number of medical men are now convinced that the LAW OF DESTINY is an important factor in producing disease and retarding recover, though they are not believers in the fallacy of an inexorable fate. They recognize that GOD DOES NOT WILLINGLY AFFLICT US NOR AIM TO GET EVEN WITH THE TRANSGRESSOR; they understand that all sorrow and suffering are designed to teach us lessons which we would not or could not learn in any other way. The stars show the period estimated as requisite to teach us the lesson, but EVEN GOD CANNOT DETERMINE THE EXACT TIME not the amount of suffering necessary; we, ourselves, have a prerogative,

FOR WE ARE DIVINE. If we awake to our transgression and commence to obey the law ere the stellar affliction ceases, we are cured of our mental, moral, or physical distemper; if we persist to the end of one stellar affliction without having learned our lesson, a more inimical configuration will enforce obedience at a later time.

It is in this connection that the spiritually minded health adjuster may often render most efficient service and shorten the period of suffering by pointing out to a sufferer why he is afflicted. Even when the healer finds himself unable to cope with the disease, he may very often cheer a patient through a period of unavoidable distress by a promise of relief at a certain time. In my ministrations to the sick during bygone years it has not infrequently been my privilege to thus point out the Star of Hope, and, so far as I remember, my predictions of recovery at a set time have always been verified, sometimes in an almost miraculous manner, for THE STARS ARE THE CLOCK OF DESTINY AND ARE ALWAYS CORRECT.

In the above you have the great reason why we should study astrology from the spiritual standpoint. In next month's letter I hope to bring out something more definite concerning the Spiritual Panacea, but in the meantime I am sure you will be glad to know that we have bought the land of which I spoke. It is one of the sightliest spots in beautiful southern California; in fact, though I have traveled all over the world, I have never seen a view to compare with that of the site of our future Headquarters. It is situated upon a high tableland, giving free scope to the vision for forty or more miles in all directions. On the north the Santa Ana Mountain Range wards off the cold north winds so that the climate is practically frostless all the year round. Below us to the east is the beautiful San Luis Rey Valley, with its river like a silver band wending it way through fertile fields past the historic old Spanish Mission where the Franciscan Fathers taught the Indians for centuries. Farther eastward the San Jacinto mountain rears its snow-capped peak against a sky of deepest azure. In the south the promontory of La Jolla, with its picturesque caves, hides from view the great natural harbor of Uncle Sam's southwesternmost city--San Diego. Towards the setting sun we behold upon the placid bosom of the Pacific Ocean, San Clemente Island, also Santa Catalina with its wonderful submarine gardens--a composite picture of glory and inspiration, in itself sufficient to evoke all that is purest and best in any one at all spiritually inclined.

We have named this beauty spot of nature, "Mt. Ecclesia," and a building fund has already been started to erect suitable buildings: a School of Healing, a Sanitarium, and last but not least, a place of worship--an Ecclesia, where the Spiritual Panacea may be prepared and sent all over the world to be used by properly qualified helpers.

BAPTISM OF WATER AND OF SPIRIT

LAST month we started to consider the sacraments, and it was my intention to write upon COMMUNION this month, but the subject has proved so vast that it takes in almost everything from Genesis to Revelation, besides a number of physiological aspects such as the chemistry of good and the blood; also the atmosphere, etc. Further, it is inseparably connected with the second coming of Christ. It will require more time than I can give to get it out early in the month, also it will cover several lessons. Therefore I thought it best not to use that subject until next month, and in the meantime I have decided to give you a lesson from the new book--THE ROSICRUCIAN MYSTERIES. This lesson is partly taken from the chapter entitled, "The Mystery of Light, Color, and Consciousness." You will find it most interesting and instructive.

Regarding last month's lesson on BAPTISM, you will have noted that so far from being only an outgrowth of the dogmatism commonly attributed to the church, it is the symbol of condition which actually existed in the past when humanity was indeed a brotherhood. It is a fact of the greatest significance that until the time of Christ, the LAW demanded an eye for an eye and a tooth for a tooth, but ere He commenced to preach the gospel of LOVE to our neighbor and forgiveness towards those who trespass against us, He went under the Waters of Baptism, and there received the Universal Spirit, which will supplant the egoism of today.

Thus He became filled with love, and therefore NATURALLY radiated that quality, as naturally as a stove filled with burning coal radiates heat. We may preach to the stove forever that its duty is to heat, but until we fill it with fuel, it will remain cold. Likewise, we may preach to humanity that we ought to be brothers and love one another, but until we put ourselves "IN TUNE WITH THE INFINITE," we can no more love our neighbor than the empty stove can heat. As Paul says, "Though I speak with the tongues of men and of angles, and have not LOVE, I am become as sounding brass, or a tinkling cymbal." THE BAPTISM OF WATER refers to a past condition when we were irresponsible as the child we take to church today, but THE BAPTISM OF SPIRIT is something yet in the future for most of us, and it is this for which we are striving. Let us pay particular attention to the thirteenth chapter of 1st Corinthians during this coming month. Let us endeavor to practice in our daily lives at least one of the virtues which Paul says lead to illumination, so that we may soon fit ourselves to see face to face the beauties of the sacraments, which perhaps are now but dimly perceived as through a darkened glass.

RULING OUR STARS

I hope you enjoyed last month's lesson on "The Mystery of Light, Color and Consciousness," and that you now have a more thorough realization of what is meant by the saying, "In Him we live and move and have our being," for everywhere, throughout the whole universe, wherever light penetrates, there God also is. Even in the places which WE call dark because the constitution of our eyes prevents perception of objects there, organs of vision differently constituted can function as exemplified in the instance of cats and owls.

Christ said, "Let your light shine." To the spiritual vision each human being appears as a flame of light, variously colored according to temperament, and or greater or less brilliancy in proportion to purity of character. Science has discovered that all matter is in a state of flux, that the particles which compose our bodies continually decay and are eliminated from the system, to be replaced by others which remain for a short time until they also decompose. Likewise our moods, emotions, and desires change with every passing moment, the old giving place to the new in an interminal succession. Therefore, they also must be composed of matter and subject to laws similar to those which govern visible physical substances.

We even can, and do, change our mind; we can cultivate it in one direction or another as we please, just as we can develop the muscles of arm or limb, or we can allow the member to atrophy. Therefore the mind also must be composed of a changeable substance. But the ego, the Thinker, never loses its "I"-dentity. In both childhood and old age that "I" remains the same regardless of changes in thoughts, feelings, emotions, and desires. Though the body, which we use as a garment, changes with the passing years, WE are eternally and everlasting the same.

The quality of mutability of matter and evanescence of form is the basis of all spiritual progress, however, for it matter were immutable as spirit, there would be no possibility of advancement. So long as we drift with the tide of life and do not consciously control the ebb and flow of matter to and from our being, we are the sport of circumstances. Then when a ray of Mars is projected at a certain angle to the atoms of our body, we feel all the aggressiveness which it carries. A Saturnian beam, on the other hand, brings us depression; it fills us with gloom and fearful forebodings. But as we evolve and arrive at an understanding of the MYSTERY OF LIGHT, COLOR, AND CONSCIOUSNESS, we gradually learn to rule our stars. Then by conformity to the laws of nature we become masters of our own destiny; and it is of vital importance that no matter what the aspects which may rule at any certain time we should always assert ourselves and say:

"It matters not how strait the gate,
How charged with punishments the scroll,
'I' am the master of my fate;
'I' am the captain of my soul."

INVISIBLE GUARDIANS OF HUMANITY

YOU saw in the lesson, on Baptism, how we went back to the earliest days of evolution upon our planet to find the significance of that sacrament. You will have noticed also in last month's lesson how the Sacrament of Communion has its root in the beginning of time. Thus it is apparent that unless we are capable of investigating the past history of the human race, we can obtain no clear conception concerning anything connected with mankind. Goethe spoke of "DAS EWIG WERDENDE"-the ever becoming. Change is the mainspring of progression, and if we look upon man AS HE IS NOW, without regard to what he has been, our deductions as to his future must necessarily be very limited.

The last lesson illustrates the Law of Analogy, showing how man was fostered by Divine Guardians in a manner similar to that in which the little child is care for by its parents to prepare it for the battle of life; and we may be sure that though these guardians have withdrawn from VISIBLE leadership, they are still with us and keep a watchful eye upon their former wards, just as we who are parents continue to take an interest in the welfare of our children after they have left our hearth and home to fight the battle of life for themselves.

When we have had our spiritual eyes opened and have learned to distinguish the various classes of beings in the higher realms, that guardianship is one of the most reassuring facts to the observer; for though no one may interfere with the free will of mankind and though it is contrary to the divine plan in any way to coerce a man into doing that which he does not want to do, there is no bar against suggestions along lines which he would be likely to choose. And it is due to the wisdom and love of these Great Beings that progress along humanitarian lines is the watchword of the day.

During the ages which have passed, we in the Western world have particularly felt the sorrow and pain due to war and strife. The struggle for existence is constantly becoming more and more acute; it is dictated by "man's inhumanity to man." But there is also another factor developed by the Lords of Love and Compassion, namely, the altruistic movements, which are multiplying in number at a wonderful rate, and gaining in efficiency as the years go by. it is a noteworthy fact, however, that alms-giving and charity which degrade the recipient are being more and more superseded by HELP TO SELF-HELP, which elevates who we aid as well as those who give.

That kind of help involves thought and self-sacrifice, which are fostered by our Invisible Guardians among the stronger who are now their weaker brothers' keepers.

It is a cause for considerable congratulation that a number of our Fellowship members are workers in institutions conducted along the above lines, and I sincerely hope to see the day when a large majority will be able to take up work of this nature, each in his respective environment. But begin at home, be kind to all with whom you immediately come in contact, and when you have been found faithful in a few things, the larger opportunities will not be wanting.

FLESH FOOD AND ALCOHOL

IT is one of the usual human characteristics to eulogize that which pleases us, and deprecate that for which we have an aversion, but I trust that you will have learned from last month's lesson the one great and glorious fact that IN THE FATHER'S KINGDOM ALL THINGS WORK TOGETHER FOR GOOD. Those among us who are content to live upon vegetables, and those among us who feel no desire for strong drink, are usually too prone to look down upon our brothers and sisters who still use flesh food and intoxicants with a feeling of, "I am so much holier that thou"; but you will doubtless have perceived from what has been said in the lesson that such a feeling is entirely gratuitous. Flesh food and alcohol have had a very material share in the world's progress, and were it not for them we should not today be enjoying many of the comforts and labor-saving devices which make life in the Western world so much easier than in primeval times. Neither is the day of their usefulness entirely past; they are necessities in the lives of many people. Besides, as the Good Book says, it is not that which goes into the mouth that defiles, but that which proceeds therefrom; and the attitude of haughty disdain for those who still use flesh foods, or are subject to alcoholism, is far more subversive of spiritual growth than the mere partaking of these foods.

Let us therefore not condemn others, but let us try to see the matter from their side, and allow them to have their free will as we wish to have ours. Neither let us obtrude our views upon them nor seek to make converts to our mode of living among those who are not yet ready. THE CHANGE OUGHT TO COME FROM WITHIN, and it should not be dictated by a consideration of the healthfulness of vegetable food, nor by the spiritual acceleration to be gained from a diet prepared without flesh. The highest motive should be compassion for the poor victims which are slain to appease appetites.

It may be said, however, with safety that we eat too much flesh, and like all compounds of nitrogen, such as nitro-glycerine, gun-cotton, and other explosives, flesh foods are extremely unstable and dangerous to the system. Therefore we will do well if we urge moderation upon all with whom we come in contact. Science is sufficiently well aware of the facts in the case to furnish ample backing for any one who undertakes this mission. We may not save the lives of as many animals by preaching moderation among our associates as we would if we could convert them to a bloodless diet, but if our motive is to avert tragedy to all possible, that will be the wisest course. Also is we can inculcate a spirit of compassion, the desire for flesh will soon vanish before the spirit of love.

PREPARATIONS FOR REMOVAL TO MT. ECCLESIA

SATURDAY, October the 28th, at 12:40 P.M. sharp, Pacific time, we are going to break ground for the first building on Mt. Ecclesia, the home-site of the Rosicrucian Fellowship. The house will be comparatively small, and we are striving to make it as inexpensive or we shall not be able to build at all. I am even doing the work of architect and contractor to save expenses. Nevertheless, we consider this first breaking of ground an epoch of greatest import in the young life of our society, for though our private quarters may be cramped we shall have a large workroom and accommodation for several assistants until funds become available for erection of the Ecclesia and other pretentious structures more worthy of our mission in the world.

We realize most keenly that the magnitude of our work in the world depends in a large measure upon the support and co-operation of our associates, and we therefore most earnestly solicit your active assistance upon this momentous occasion, to the end that our society may become a greater power for good than any which has gone before.

You know that thoughts are things; that they are forces of a magnitude proportionate to the intensity of purpose behind them. There is no easier or more effective method of putting our whole being in tune with a certain design, and hurling a powerful thought in a desired direction, than earnest Christian prayer.

Now, I have two distinct requests for your help in prayer, and I hope and trust you will give your most hearty support.

In the first place, though altogether unworthy, it will be my duty as leader to break the ground for our future Headquarters at the time set, and it is is possible for you to withdraw to your closet, please give yourself up to earnest prayer that the Headquarters then being started may grown and prosper in every good way; for the united prayers of our students all over the world will be an immense force in that direction.

But you can do more; the cumulative thought of many friends directed day by day towards a common center will work wonders. Will you send us a prayer every night to strengthen Mrs. Heindel, the workers at Headquarters, and myself, so that we may grow purer, better, and more efficient workers in the service of humanity, and that we may thus become more potent to alleviate the sorrow, suffering, and distress of all who seek our aid? Further, will you write me once in a while assuring me of your sympathy and co-operation? I may not be able to reply and thank you individually, but you can rest assured that I shall appreciate your expression of good will none the less.

GROUND-BREAKING FOR FIRST BUILDING ON

MT. ECCLESIA This month I am departing from my usual custom of devoting the student's letter entirely to a review of the previous months lesson, in order to tell you of the ceremony we had at Mt.Ecclesia on the 28th, when we broke ground for the first building on the site of our permanent Headquarters. I feel sure you were with us in spirit, that you are eager to hear about it, and I know the recital will bring us in closer touch.

Our first idea was to forego any outward show or ceremony. We desired to avoid all unnecessary expense as our funds are not, even now, sufficient to finish the building inside, and we shall have to rough it for awhile until conditions are more favorable.

I had intended to go there and hold the service mentally, and alone, but it seemed so cold, dreary, and desolate not to have one friend there in person to rejoice with me on that momentous occasion, not even my dear companion in the work-Mrs. Heindel. Moreover, as this is a very important affair of the Rosicrucian Fellowship and not a personal matter, I felt that opportunity to attend ought to be given the members. The thought grew upon me until I decided to ask the Teacher's advice; and, as he most heartily approved, we made an appropriation for the purpose of celebrating the event in a simple, yet fitting manner, and sent notices to friends in the immediate vicinity.

We made a large cross of the same style as our emblem, and on the three upper ends we had painted, in gilt letters, the initials: C R C. These, you know, represent the symbolical name of our great Head, and designate our emblem as the Christian Rose Cross, which conveys an idea of beauty and a higher life so different from the gloom of death usually associated with the black cross.

This cross and a climbing rose we decided to plant at the same time as we broke ground for the building, so that they might symbolize the verdant life of the various kingdoms traveling to higher spheres along the spiral path of evolution.

On the 27th, Mrs. Heindel and I started for Oceanside, nearly exhausted from the strain of packing and moving. The first rain of the season was falling, and we felt some apprehension concerning the effect on the ceremony; but as we looked toward the almost cloud-hidden mountains in the east, we beheld the largest, most glorious rainbow we had ever seen-a double rainbow in fact-and it's southern foot seemed to stand directly upon Mt. Ecclesia.

Our responsibility to aid thousands of weary hearts to bravely bear their burdens has often seemed beyond our strength; yet always have we found our powers renewed by looking within; and this time it seemed as if all Nature wanted to cheer us and was saying: "Take courage, remember the Work is not yours but God's; trust entirely in Him; He will point the way." So we clasped hands and took heart with new strength to carry on the beautiful work of which Mt. Ecclesia is to be the center.

The day of the ceremony was an ideal California day; the sun shone is a cloudless sky. Wherever we looked from Mt. Ecclesia, oceans, valleys, mountains seemed to smile. Both the workers and visiting members were enraptured with the incomparable beauty of the Headquarters site. Those present were: Annie R. Atwood, of San Diego; Ruth E. Beach, of Portland, Ore.; Rachel M. Cunningham, Rudolf Miller and John Adams of Los Angeles; George Kramer, of Pittsburgh, Pa; Wm. M. Patterson, of Seattle, Wash.; Mrs. Heindel and myself.

At the appointed time I broke ground for the building. All helped to excavate for the cross, which was set by Wm. Patterson. Mrs. Heindel planted the rose, which was then watered by all present. May it grow, may it bloom, to adorn the nakedness of the cross and be an inspiration to purity of life that will cover all past sins, no matter how dark the life may have been. The address--as it should have been delivered-constitutes this month's lesson. Circumstances occasioned some modifications.

GENERATIVE PURITY THE IDEAL FOR THE WEST.

HAVE you grasped the main point in our last month's lesson on the symbolism of the Rose Cross, the crux of the Western Wisdom Teaching? It is Generative Purity.

The great Leaders of humanity always prescribe conditions most conducive to the growth of each race; different religions for the masses, and varying methods of attainment for the few. The populous condiion of the far East proves a universally unrestricted indulgence of the passions upon the part of our younger Chinese and Hindu brothers. Therefore the Wisdom Teachers of the East prescribe celibacy for their disciples as a means of gaining control over passion.

In the West conditions are more complicated and dangerous. Here the floodgates of passion are, in a large measure, dammed up; not from a sense of the sanctity of the generative act, but because of selfishness and fancied economic necessity. This method often leads to insidious perversion and loose practices. Were not passion so strong, this method might indeed result in race suicide. To require an aspirant born under such conditions to live a celibate life would only given him further incentive to selfish ness and self-sufficiency; so it is regarded as a mark of merit when a pupil of the Western Mystery School marries and continues to live a life of chastity.

It has been a detriment to the Western world that various societies have promulgated Eastern doctrines-celibacy among others-here, and it was a severe shock to me when an officer in one such organization deplored the marriage of one of their lecturers, and told how it had embarrassed them that his wife was about to be confined. As the years brought new additions to the family the society has since relegated him to private life.

The exact reverse would have happened to pupils of the Western School. They are most highly honored if able and willing to give a body and a home to one or more waiting spirits, provided, of course, that they live a life of chaste conjugal love during the intervals.

Thus while the younger, weaker Eastern soul is commanded by the Compassionate Teachers, who temper the wind to the short lamb, to be celibate and flee temptation, the older Western spirit is allowed to test its strength by living in conjugal relations and perchance in accomplishing an immaculate conception such as symbolized by the chaste, beautiful rose which scatters its seed without passion, without shame.

A New Race is being born now. Pure-minded Christian men and women are awakening more and more to the claims of the unborn. Let us celebrate the anniversary of our Savior's birth by praying that pure conditions may soon become general, and that all children may be well-born. Last, but not least, let each of us teach, preach, and live this doctrine.

THE COMING AGE OF AIR

REVIEWING last month's lesson, there is the startling statement that in the next epoch we shall abandon our present terra firma and live in the air clothed in a gaseous body. Another writer along these lines has provoked much amusement by a series of articles so wildly imaginary that the opinions which we have heard expressed unanimously vote him champion among story tellers. Yet he stays on earth; his temples are as solid as a rock; and I have hesitated to publish the above mentioned teaching till I decided that duty required me to speak, even if some students do class me as visionary.

The trouble is, we have all become so much more impregnated with materialism than we realize, and it hinders us in our quest. As students of transcendental philosophy, we have accustomed ourselves to regard individual and intermittent life in a ethereal body possible attainment for the few, but that the whole human race may live permanently for a whole epoch in the air!--truly, it made me hold my breath when I realized that the Bible means exactly what it says when it states that WE SHALL MEET THE LORD IN THE AIR AND BE WITH HIM FOR THE AGES.

Looking towards the future through the perspective of the past, however, the idea should really cause no surprise for it is strictly in line with the path whence we have come to our present development. We lived at one time like the mineral and were imbedded in the gaseous earth. We grew outwards from the fiery core during a plantlike existence. Our peregrinations commenced upon the thin earth crust at a later time; and we are now upon the highlands of the earth, far from the inner core where our evolution commenced. The march of progression has been OUTWARDS all the while, and it follows that the next step ought to raise us above the earth level.

I am giving this teaching out for consideration because the majority of our students believe in rebirth and the Law of Consequence, which are the main arbiters of destiny during the present dispensation of recurring cycles. Knowledge of these laws is of great value as it enables us to order our life intelligently, building in THIS LIFE the conditions of the NEXT EMBODIMENT.

The majority of Christians have not this great advantage, but they live, never the less, through all the tribulations of THIS AGE--the Kingdom of Men-in the grand hope that they may qualify for admission the the Kingdom of God--THE NEXT AGE. Our view of life has a SHORTER, theirs, a LONGER, focus. They live less scientifically than those among us who apply our more exact knowledge of present conditions, but they are fitting themselves for the FUTURE Age if they LIVE by the Bible. Their information may be vague, but they live and die in the firm belief of the great and cardinal truth that they will GO TO HEAVEN and be with THE LORD FOREVER if they are real Christians.

If we believe ONLY in rebirth, we can expect nothing but a continuous RETURN TO EARTH to battle with the LAW of Jehovah; we have no part in the LOVE of Christ. To be perfectly in line with the facts, to be able to live by THE WHOLE TRUTH, we must realize that birth and death are evanescent features of this age of concrete existence, but LIFE ITSELF IS INTERMINABLE. John tells us very definitely that though it does not appear what our constitution shall be, we shall be changed to the likeness of Christ and remain deathless throughout the Age; and it behooves us to keep this great hope firmly before us and pray for the Kingdom to come, as our Lord taught.

THE ROLE OF STIMULANTS IN EVOLUTION

OUR last lesson finished the series dealing with the sacrament of Communion by description of how the spirit alcohol, which is fermented OUTSIDE the system, is being superseded by sugar, which ferments WITHIN. I trust you to see the thread of the argument which has been running through these lessons: That a stimulant from the lethargy attendant upon a meat diet; that the bacchanalian orgies in ancient temples, which properly fill us with horror nowadays, were the on immense value in human development; that the first miracle of Christ and His Last Supper were devoted to a dispensation of the stimulant; the He ordained its use "till He come"; that as consumption of sugar increases, use of alcohol diminishes and, concurrently, the moral standard is gradually elevated; that people grow more altruistic and Christlike in proportion to their use of the non-inebriating stimulant, and that therefore the temperance movement is one of the most powerful factors to hasten the coming of Christ.

But as we cultivate finer and more delicate feelings, we shall shrink in horror also from flesh food; and some day it will be considered as morbid a taste to desire to use the stomach as a receptacle for the corpses of killed animals as it now adjudged by society a morbid taste to desire strong drink inordinately. As students of the Western Wisdom Teaching we should not judge, however, but recognize the fact that many really require these articles in moderation; but the matter is being adjusted by the invisible leaders of evolution in a manner not yet obvious to casula observers, though it is quite discernible to deeper investigators.

It is evident that evolutionary progress is elevating the lower kingdoms as well as humanity. The animals, particularly the domesticated species, are nearing individualization, and their withdrawal from manifestation has already commenced. As a result it will in time be possible to obtain flesh food. Then the death knell of "King Alcohol" will have struck, for only flesh eaters crave liquor.

In the meantime plant life is growing more sentient. The lateral limbs of trees produce more abundantly than do vertical branches because in plants, as in us, consciousness results from the antagonistic activities of the desire and vital currents. Lateral limbs are swept through their entire length by the desire currents which circle our planet and which act so powerfully in the horizontal animal spines. The desire currents rouse the sleeping plant life in the lateral limbs to a higher degree of consciousness than is the case with the vertical currents radiating from the center of the earth. Thus, in time, the plants will also become too sensitive to serve as food and another source must be sought.

Today, we have considerable ability in working with the chemical, mineral substances; we mold them into houses, ships, and all the other things which evidence our civilization. We are master of the minerals OUTSIDE our body, but powerless to assimilate and use them INSIDE our system to build our organs until the plant life has transmuted crystals into crystalloids. Our work with the minerals in the exterior world is raising their vibration and is paving the way for direct interior use. By spiritual alchemy we shall build the temple of the spirit, conquer the dust whence we came, and qualify as true Master Masons prepared for work in higher spheres.

NECESSITY FOR DEVOTION

AS the subject of marriage, with which our last month's lesson dealt, is in certain sense receiving a further treatment this month, I feel that the letter to students this month may perhaps be most profitably devoted to a point on which I have for a long time wished to speak.

The ROSICRUCIAN COSMO-CONCEPTION has met with such phenomenal success and called forth so much gratitude and admiration all over the world that I ought to be flattered at the attention it is commanding everywhere. But, on the contrary, I am beginning to feel more and more afraid that the book may miss the mark at which our Elder Brothers have aimed. Its purpose, designated on pages 17 and 18, is to satisfy the mind by intellectually explaining the world mystery, so that the devotional side of the student's nature may be allowed to develop along lines which the intellect has approved. The ROSICRUCIAN COSMO-CONCEPTION, I believe, has won its way because of this appeal to the intellect and the satisfaction it has given to the inquiring mind. Hundreds, yes thousands, of letters have testified that students who have searched in vain for years have found here what they sought. But few have seemed able, as yet, to transcend the intellectual conception, and unless the book gives the student an earnest desire to transcend the path of knowledge and pursue the path of devotion it is a failure, in my estimation.

In another society formed along these lines, I have known groups to sit in classes for years wrangling before a chart of the atom, delving deep into the minutiae of its spirals and spirillae, but cold and indifferent to the woe of the world around them; and it is with great sorrow deepening apprehension that I note the development of a tendency in that direction among some of our students, a tendency in that direction among some of our students, a tendency which I hope may be checked before it kills the heart. "Knowledge puffeth up, but love edifieth," says Paul, and this is well exemplified in the attitude of leaders in the society to which I have reference, who often belittle the Christian religion on the platform or in print because it lacks an intellectual conception of the universe.

Let me recall to you the warning given by our Teacher in the ROSICRUCIAN COSMO-CONCEPTION with reference to diagrams: "They are at best only crutches to aid our limited faculties; when we make a diagram to explain spiritual mysteries, it is as if we should take the wheels out of a watch and lay them side by side to illustrate how the watch keeps time." Although charts may be a valuable help at a certain stage of our development, it behooves us always to remember their limitations and STRIVE TO ATTAIN BY OUR INTUITION the true spiritual idea. I feel also that it is of the greatest importance that students should keep the true purpose of the COSMO-CONCEPTION, its aim and its end, most clearly and accurately before them at all times. It is stated in black letter son the return postal cards, and I would advise every student to write it in LARGE letters and past it into the ROSICRUCIAN COSMO-CONCEPTION where it may be seen each time the book is opened, for though we have all knowledge and can solve all mysteries, we are but as tinkling cymbals unless we have love and USE IT to help our fellow creatures.

STRAGGLERS IN EVOLUTION

FROM the teaching contained in last month's lesson you will understand that there is absolutely not foundation for the idea, as commonly held, about lost souls. There is not a single word in the Bible which carries with it the idea that we have become accustomed to associate with the English word "forever." The Greek word is AIONIAN and means "an indefinite period of time, an age"; and when we read in the Bible the words, "forever and ever" they should really be translated "for ages and ages." Besides, as it is a truth in nature that "in God we live and move and have our being," a soul lost would mean that a part of God would be lost, and that of course is unthinkable.

Since writing last month's lesson another point has occurred to me which will illustrate how the "lost" of one Period are dealt with in the next.

You remember that we have spoken of the Lucifer spirits as stragglers from the Moon Period and that we stated that they could find no field of evolution in the present scheme of manifestation. The archangels inhabit the sun, the angels have charge of all the moons, but the Lucifer spirits were incapable of dwelling upon either luminary. They could not assist in generation purely and unselfishly as do the angels, but were actuated by passion and selfish desires, so that a separate place had to be found for them. Therefore they were placed upon the planet Mars, a fact well known to the ancient astrologers who have Mars rule over Aries, which has dominion over the head (remember, the brain is built by subverted sex force), and also gave that planet rule over Scorpio, which governs the reproductive organs. Aries is the 1st house in a flat horoscope, denoting the beginning of life; Scorpio is the 8th, signifying death; and therein is contained the lesson that all which is generated by passion and desire is bound to meet dissolution. Thus Mars is, astrologically and estorecially, "the devil"; and Lucifer, the chief among fallen angles, is truly the adversary of Jehovah, who directs the fecundating force from the sun through the lunar agency.

Nevertheless, the Lucifer Spirits are aiding in the process of evolution. From them we received the iron which alone makes it possible to live in an oxygenated atmosphere. They have been, and are, agitators for material progress, and we have no right to anathematize them. The Bible distinctly forbids us to revile the gods. Jude states that not even the archangel Michael dared revile Lucifer, and in the Book of Job the latter is spoken of as among the sons of God. His ambassador to the earth, Samuel, is the angel of death, signified by Scorpio, but is also the angel of life and action symbolized by Aries. Were it not for the stirring martial impulses we might not feel sorrow as keenly as we do, but neither could we make the same progress, and surely "it is better to wear out than to rust out." Thus you see how these "lost sheep" of a former age are given a change to retrieve their estate in the present scheme of evolution. They are delayed, and, as stragglers, must always appear evil, but they are not "lost beyond redemption." They may save themselves by serving us, probably by transmuting Scorpio into Aries, generation into regeneration.

KEYNOTE OF THE ROSICRUCIAN TEACHINGS

THE burden of last month's lesson was that it is our duty to pass on the fruits of our study in an endeavor to benefit the world. But mystics usually stand aloof from their fellows and the world looks askance at us and our beliefs. This ought not to be, and analysis will prove that the teachings objected to are relatively unimportant and that the most vital of the teachings will find ready acceptance and prepare the way for further instructions.

The value of any particular teaching depends upon its power to make men better HERE and NOW; to make them kind and considerate at home, conscientious in business, loyal to friends, forgiving to enemies; and any teaching which is easily applied, and will accomplish such results, need no further recommendation.

Where shall we look for such a teaching? We have a monumental cosmogony, describing world periods, revolutions, epochs, and races. Will that study make men more kind? Or, if we can get them to pore over the mystery of numbers and names in the Kabala, will they become more conscientious? Surely not; therefore such knowledge is of minor import. Will it make men moral if we teach them of involution and evolution, or if we describe the cyclic journey of the soul through purgatory and heaven? It will not necessarily, at least till we have convinced them that under the Law of Consequence we are subject to rebirth, and reap as we sow. Even a hint of such a belief, however, would turn most people from us.

But, you will ask, what them is left of our teachings? The greatest teaching of all, and the most practical. One that will arouse no antagonism in any devotee of any religion, or even in an agnostic, for it need not be labeled religious. It will produce most beneficent results from the day it is applied, and affect future lives also, regardless of whether the man who practices it ever hears the word Rosicrucian or learns more of our teachings.

If you want to really work in God's vineyard--the world--don't isolate yourself. Abstract study may be good part of the time, but go out in the world; win the confidence of people in church, club, or shop. If you set a good example, they will inquire the secret, and you will be privileged to give them the greatest teaching ever known: THE SECRET OF SOUL GROWTH You may talk to them something like this: "Every night when I have gone to bed I review the happenings of the day IN REVERSE ORDER. I try to judge myself impartially. I blame where blame is due, repent, and resolve to reform. I praise myself, it praise is merited, and determine to do better next day.

"I fail often to keep my good resolutions, BUT I KEEP ON TRYING, and little by little I succeed." It may be well to explain that by reviewing events in reverse order they are more firmly implanted in the memory, but further elucidation should be avoided until you are certain your friend is seeking a solution to the problem of life.

This is discriminative propaganda.

SACREDNESS OF SPIRITUAL EXPERIENCES

MANY letters have been received during the past month voicing appreciation of students in respect to the last lessons, and it has been a source of gratification to note the deep-felt love for the Fellowship and the desire to know "how it all came about." Thus I feel somewhat better about introducing my personal experiences than I did in the first place.

At the same time it cannot be too strongly emphasized that indiscriminate relating of superphysical experiences is one of the most harmful of practices, no matter from what standpoint we look at it. In Lecture No. 11, "Spiritual Sight and Insight," the matter has been thoroughly explained. The "treasure-trove" must be lifted in silence; and from the Greek myth we learn that Tantalus was hurled down into the infernal regions for divulging spiritual secrets. In other words, we cannot attain true illumination while we go hawking our dreams and visions from pillar to post and recount them even to people manifestly unwilling to listen. Thereby we profane and cheapen what we ought to reverence, and the desecration is apt to focus our vision in the infernal regions, the lower strata of the desire world.

Again, such recitals always tax the credulity of those to whom they are related. There is not measure whereby we may gauge their accuracy. They often seem to have no practical bearing upon the problem of life; and even if we have faith in the veracity of the visionary, there is not value in his stories unless we can find an underlying law or purpose. Thus the statement of the law is sufficient without embellishment. Perhaps, the best illustration of this point may be given by relating how I discovered the law of infant mortality which was never published till it appeared in our literature.

My Teacher one day set me the task of following a certain person's life through two previous embodments and reporting. I had no idea that I was being sent in quest of a law, but thought the purpose was to develop my faculty of reading the Memory of Nature. When ready, I reported the result to my Teacher who inquired particularly the circumstances attending death in each of the two lives. I answered that the man died in battle the first time and from sickness as a child the last. That was correct, and another person's life was given me to investigate. That one died in bed the first time, and also died as a child the last time. A third person's life terminated in a fire the first time, and seemingly also as a child the last time. I say "seemingly," for I could scarcely believe the evidence of my senses, and felt diffident when I reported to my Teacher. I was surprised when he said I was correct. This feeling grew as I, in turn investigated fourteen person's lives. IN the first life they died under varying circumstances; some in battle, others by accidents, and others in bed surrounded by weeping relatives; but in the second life all passed out as children.

The Teacher then told me to compare these lives to find why they died as children, and for many weeks I studied them night after night, but could find not similarity in the conditions of their first death until one Sunday morning just as I was entering my body, it flashed through my brain. I awoke with a shout--Eureka! I almost jumped into the middle of the floor in my joy at having found the key. The horrors of battle, fire, and accident, and the lamentations of relatives alike prevent deep etching of the life-panorama; and the value of a life terminated under such conditions would be lost save for the following death as a child and subsequent tuition first in the first heaven, a fully elucidated in our literature. The law, as there stated, logically explains a mystery of life independent of the accuracy of my story. As I relate it only to give point to our lesson, I feel consistent when exhorting others to silence as to their spiritual experiences.

INITIATIVE AND PERSONAL FREEDOM

WHAT do you think is the main point in last month's lesson? It is not MY experiences, although students have attached a great deal of worth to them, but in reality they are insignificant save as they serve to convey teaching of benefit part from them. The greatest value of that which was recorded in last month's lesson is the reiterated and emphatic insistence on absolute PERSONAL FREEDOM in the Rosicrucian Fellowship.

In this respect the Western Mystery Teaching differs most radically from that given to the younger souls of the East, where each has his Master--a despot whom he slavishly serves in all things as "Kim" did the Guru he followed, for there is considerable truth and fact in Kipling's story. There, absolute and unquestioning obedience to the command of the EXTERIOR Master he sees and serves physically is the means of spiritual advancement; the pupil is entirely without choice or prerogative, but neither has be responsibility.

Among the older souls of the WEST who aspire to spiritual growth, there can be no Master or Guide. We are to learn to stand alone. We may not like it; we may be afraid, and want a Master or Guide to free ourselves from responsibility. In that fact lies the reason, I think, why so many intelligent and cultured people have joined spiritualistic circles and societies promulgating Eastern teachings. Advanced beyond normal Western development, they sense the Great Beyond, and it draws them as the wide expanse of blue sky draws the nestling, despite fears, to trust its untried wings; but the inward urge compels; and, fearing to trust themselves, they grasp eagerly at the hand of "Masters" or "Spirit Guides" in the hope of attaining spiritual power by their help. But the baby must crawl and fall; it must rise, fall again and hurt itself. The experience is unpleasant but unavoidable, and far to be preferred to the consequences of tying the infant to a chair to save it from falling; then its limbs would become useless. And so do the latent spiritual powers of the unfortunates who come under the (to Westerners) baneful domination of Spirit Guides and Eastern Masters.

The Western Teacher is more like the parent bird which pushes the young off the nest if they do not go themselves. We may hurt ourselves, but WE DO LEARN TO FLY. Take my own case: Pushed out in the world with the Rosicrucian teaching and told to spread it, you may be sure I have held by breath many a time as the realization grew of what a gigantic undertaking it is, and how insignificant Mrs. Heindel and I are. Often, when the work seemed about to swamp us, we have prayed and prayed for help, but as we look back we can see what lessons we have learned by the struggle. Sometimes frined have remarked: "Oh, how we wish the money would be forthcoming to build the Ecclesia and schools, so that the work might be carried into the world with greater effect"; but we realize that there are other lessons before us, and that when we are ready, the means for further extension will come; until then, our wings need more training.

It is the same with every associate of the Fellowship. We are to learn the lesson of working for a common purpose, without leadership; each prompted alike by the Spirit of Love from within to strive for the physical, moral, and spiritual uplift of all the world so the stature of Christ--THE LORD AND LIGHT OF THE WORLD.

THE CHRIST SPIRIT AND THE SPIRITUAL PANACEA

YOU remember reading in the ROSICRUCIAN COSMO-CONCEPTION about how in the ages from Noah to Christ, under the regime of Jehovah, universal selfishness was fostered in the entire human race. Man was told that "Heaven, even the heavens, are the Lord's, but the earth has He given to the children of men." Thus man was urged to seek material possessions, and had no conception of treasures in heaven, which are the fruits of self-sacrifice. As a consequence, his heaven life became more and more barren; spiritual progress waned, and unless a new impulse had been given, it must eventually have ceased.

Then the Cosmic Christ Spirit, the "Redeemer," commenced His beneficent work, and eventually obtained access to the earth through the "cleansing blood of Jesus" when it flowed on Golgotha; and now the Christ Spirit is working from within our globe to attentuate its physical and superphysical constituents. An enormous spiritual inrush was felt at the moment He came into full possession of the earth on Golgotha; so great, indeed, that the intense light blinded the people. From that moment the principle altruism commenced to take a greater hold upon our race; we are gradually ceasing to look to our own interest alone, and are laying up treasure by an interest in the welfare of our fellow men. Had not Christ come, another moon must have been thrown off to rid us of the worst elements, but from this we are being saved by grace through sacrifice of the Cosmic Christ Spirit--a sacrifice that does not involve His death as commonly understood, but is an infusion of the earth with a higher life which enables us to live more abundantly in spirit.

In this coming of Christ to earth we have an analogy between it and the adminisering of the spiritual Panacrea, according to the law, "As above, so below." There is in every little cell of the human body a separate cell life, but over and above that is the ego which directs and controls all cells so that they act in harmony. During certain protracted illnesses the ego becomes so intent upon the suffering that it ceases to fully vivify the cells; thus bodily ailment breeds mental inaction and it may become impossible to throw off disease without a special impulse to dispel, the mental fog and start the cell activities anew. That is what the Spiritual Panacea does. As the inrushing Christ life on Golgotha commenced to dispel the shell of fear bred by inexorable law that hung like a pall about the earth; as it started the millions of human beings upon the path of peace and good will, so also when the Panacea is applied does the concentrated Christ life therein contained rush through the patient's body and infuse each cell with a rhythm that awakens the imprisoned ego from its lethargy and gives back life and health. May God grant that we shall soon be able to bring this great boon to suffering humanity.

THE MYSTIC BREAD AND WINE

IF I had asked the students to write me what--in their opinion--was the most important point in last month's lesson, what do you think would have been answered in the majority of the cases? I believe many would feel that the connection between the bread, the wine, and health was the principal idea; and perhaps I may be responsible for that view because I printed those words in bold type. But while it is of signal important that we should grasp this connection between the bread, the wine, and health, and apply it in our lives to the very utmost power of our ability, if we do so for any less reason that given by our Lord, it is essentially selfish, and will not further out development nearly as much as if we do it as He requested, "in remembrance of Him." Just look at the matter in this light, dear friend, and you will grasp the idea. Under the regime of Jehovah, selfishness crystallized the earth to such an extend that spiritual vibrations were almost stilled. Evolution was coming to a standstill, and the blood had become so impregnated with egoism that the race was in danger of degenerating. The Cosmic Christ then manifested through Jesus to save us. Cleansing the blood from egoism is the Mystery of Golgotha; it commenced when the blood of Jesus flowed, it has continued through the wars of Christian nations whenever men fought for an ideal, and will last until the horrors of war by contrast have sufficiently impressed mankind with the beauty of Brotherhood.

The Christ entered the earth on Golgotha. He is leavening the earth anew and making it responsive to spiritual vibrations, but His sacrifice was not consummated in a moment by DYING to save us in the generally accepted way. He is still GROWING AND TRAVAILING, WAITING FOR THE DAY OF LIBERATION, for the "manifestation of the sons of God"; and truly do we hasten that day every time we partake of food for our finer bodies symbolized by the mystic bread and wine. But we would be much more efficient in accelerating our own liberation and in hastening "the day of our Lord" if we always did it IN REMEMBRANCE OF HIM.

Do you remember "Sir Launfal's Vision"? It was not the size of the gift that counted; the gold coin he flung to the beggar was materially more valuable than the crust he gave later; but the coin was given in a spirit of impatience to be rid of a loathsome presence. The crust was given in rememberance of the Christ, and for His sake, and that made all the difference.

"And Sir Launfal said: 'I behold in thee,
An image of Him who died on the tree;
Thou also hast had thy crown of thorns,
Thou also hast had the world's buffets and scorns,
And to thy life were not denied

The wounds in the hands and feet and side;
Mild Mary's Son, acknowledge me;
Behold, through him I give to Thee!"

The more we cultivate the spirit of doing all things whatsoever for the sake of Christ and His Liberation, the better and the more fruitful lives we shall lead.

DESCENDING AND ASCENDING ARCS OF EVOLUTION

LOOKING over the last month's lesson, the most important points are the great antiquity and cosmic origin of the two great movements known now as Freemasony and Catholicism--movements instituted respectively by the Sons of Fire and the Sons of Water. It is true, as stated in the COSMO-CONCEPTION, that Initiation of human beings did not commence until about the middle of the Earth Period, when the fires of Lemuria were battling with the waters of Atlantis, but is is also true that the education of humanity depends upon the training their instructors have had in previous evolution. The attitude assumed by the two groups of angels has resulted in the above mentioned antagonistic movements. The fallen angels and fallen man are intimately connected with the work of the world under its temporal rulers. From Lucifer, the Spirit of Mars, comes the fiery red blood which is the vehicle of all material energy, ambition, and progress; but also, it is the vehicle of passion, which taints it and has caused it to flow until the earth is red. From Jehovah come the restraining Law and punishment for sin.

Let the diagram below represent the epochs through which the spirit descends and ascends, also the worlds and their corresponding bodies--then the relative connection of the various factors will be plain.

1st Epoch	7th Epoch
2nd Epoch	6th Epoch
3rd Epoch	5th Epoch
Bodies separated into sexes-male and female.	Spirits separated sexes--statecraft and priestcraft.

4th Epoch
(Turning Point)

In Lemuria, the land of the Third Epoch, mankind was separated into sexes--male and female. At that time they were spiritual beings reaching downwards into materiality, and the pioneers listened eagerly to the "gospel of the body" which they sensed dimly, but learned to know as time went on and the spiritual world faded from sight. Then the Lucifer Spirits were the teachers of the WOMAN (Eve), and Jehovah addressed himself to MAN (Adam). Women was then more advanced than man along material lines for we were then upon the descending are of the evolutionary path.

When the turning point was passed in the middle of the Atlantean Epoch, woman gradually become more spiritually inclined. She commenced to listen to the voice of Jehovah, and to fill the churches in an effort to satisfy spiritual aspirations; while man now expends the Martian energy along material lines originally advocated by the "Light-bringer," Lucifer.

As the white light changes color according to the angle of refraction, so also the viewpoint of the spirit changes with the sex of its vesture; but as the spirit alternates between male and female embodiments, we may readily balance the scales and take the path that most appeals to us, or combine the best path in both. Our later lessons will point the path, but we may say now that He who said, "I am the true Light," is at the end of the path-- Lucifer and Jehovah alike are but stepping-stones on THE WAY TO TRUTH AND LIFE.

THE ROSICRUCIAN FELLOWSHIP, AS SPIRITUAL CENTER

ON the 28th of last month it was a year since we broke ground for the first building on Mt Ecclesia. It was a typical California day of glorious sunshine with a cloudless sky whose deep blue vied with the azure of the Pacific Ocean visible for more than a hundred miles from where we stood on the Headquarters grounds. We were a little flock of nine, mostly visiting members. As we looked over the lovely green San Luis Rey valley towards the great snowclad mountains in the east and behold the white walls, the red tiled roof, and the gilded dome of the San Luis Rey Catholic Mission, where the Franciscan Fathers wrought and taught for centuries among Mexicans and Indians, it seemed to us an augur.

Here we were, a few enthusiasts, upon a bare piece of land, where we aimed to establish a Spiritual Center. Those ancient Fathers had stood in a similar position, better in some respects and worse in others. Modern methods and transportation facilities enable us to reach the whole world today, while their field was limited to their immediate vicinity. They were obliged to till the soil of the field as well as the soul of their flock to obtain a livelihood. They called upon their charges to perform the physical labor while they planned, and by their joint efforts a temple was erected where all might worship. In that respect they were much better off then we; their full membership was present at the seat of operations and ready to give physical help in the upbuilding of the Mission which was to them what our Headquarters are to the Rosicrucian Fellowship. But we have no wards; we claim no authority, and repudiate interference with individual freedom as much interference is diametrically opposed to the Rosicrucian teachings, which are the highest in the world. "If thou art Christ, help thyself," is flung at the candidate undergoing Initiation when he groans under the trial. No one who is a "leaner" can at the same time be a helper; each must learn to stand alone.

Our associate membership is four times as large as a year ago, and of course the work is vastly heavier--though system and machinery enable three of us who work in the office to do the work of a large staff, and paid help does the housework and gardening. But the routine work of preparing lessons and letters for the various classes, correcting examination papers, the sending each month of about 1500 individual letters to aid our students in difficulties, in addition to class letters, sometimes just swamps us. It seems as if we could not entertain another application for want of help to do the mechanical part of the work. But, miraculously, it seems, the sky suddenly clears, we invent a new method of accomplishing a certain part of the work with greater speed or less labor; and are ready for another increase; as said, we do four times more work than a year ago, with less help and less labor.

But while the Fellowship at large is thus cared for, Headquarters itself has suffered neglect. The proposed School of Healing, the Sanitarium, and, most important of all, the Ecclesia--where the Panacea is to be prepared and powerful healing services are to spread moral and physical health all over the world--all these are but germinal ideas as yet. As the cry of suffering humanity reaches us through many thousands of letters, our longing for the realization of the Brother's plans becomes more intense, so keen in fact that it seems to embody the concentrated yearning of all who have appealed to us in sorrow and suffering.

Our membership is scattered all over the world. We cannot follow the example of the Spanish padres and ask our students to make physical brick and lay it, brick upon brick, as a labor of love. I have never asked any one for a cent--the Rosicrucian Fellowship's work has been supported entirely by free-will offerings and the modest revenue accruing from the sale of my books--nor can I now make an appeal for a building fund; that must come from the hearts of friends, if at all; but feeling as we do here at Headquarters, the intense throb of pain in the world impels me to cast about for means of realizing the pain TO MAKE THE ROSICRUCIAN FELLOWSHIP HEADQUARTERS A MOST EFFICIENT SPIRITUAL CENTER.

A year ago I wrote the students stating the exact moment when we would break ground on Mt. Ecclesia and asked each to enter his closet and be with us in prayer if he could not be with us in person. It is wonderful what an uplift we felt from that united spiritual effort; the initial impulse has furthered the work to an inestimable degree during the past year, and I again feel impelled to invoke your help along similar lines.

The Christian Scientist "demonstrates" when he wishes to build edifices, and money pours into his coffers; the New Thoughter sends out a "demand"; and Christians of all denominations "pray" for funds. They all use one fundamental method, but employ different names. All wish magnificent piles of stone and glass, and they get them. I know that a place and building commensurate with the dignity of our work are necessary, but much as we need them, I cannot pray for sticks and stones nor can I ask you to do so; but I can, will, and do ask you to join me in the prayer THAT THE ROSICRUCIAN FELLOWSHIP HEADQUARTERS MAY BECOME A MOST EFFICIENT AND POWERFUL SPIRITUAL CENTER. Pray with your whole soul that the workers at Headquarters be given grace to push the work; make them a focus for your loving thoughts so we may radiate that grace back on a world hungry for just such love. In ourselves we are frail, but through your prayers and God's grace we shall be a mighty force in the world; and if we SEEK FIRST THE KINGDOM OF GOD, such trifles as building necessary for the work will follow as a matter of course without degrading prayer by making it a means of acquiring physical possessions.

THE MYSTIC MESSAGE OF CHRISTMAS

CHRISTMAS bells! Have you ever felt their magic in childhood days before doubt crept into your heart and shattered the ideals inculcated by the church? The same bell rang for church on Sundays and for prayer meeting at mid-week, but there was a different ring at Christmas, something unusually festive, something which we now attribute to childish imagination. We miss this something, however much we may congratulate ourselves upon emancipation from what we are pleased to term "the mummeries of the church." Wordsworth, in his "Ode to Immortality," voiced the keen feeling of regret due to loss of childish ideals; nothing the world has to give can take their place, and however we may be blessed with material wealth we are truly poor when the "glamour" of youth has gone and intellectual conceptions stifle much so-called "superstitions." Paul exhorted us to be always ready with a reason for our faith, and there is a mystic reason for many practices of the church which have been handed down from hoary antiquity. The sounding of the bell when the candle is lit upon the altar was inaugurated by spiritually illumined seers to teach the cosmic units of LIGHT and SOUND. The metal tongue of the bell bring Christ; mystic message to mankind as clearly today as when He first enunciated the graceful invitation: "Come unto me, all ye that labor and are heavy laden, and I will give you rest." Thus the bell is a symbol of Christ, "The Word," when it calls us from work to worship before the illuminated altar where He meets us as "The Light of the World." Also the particularly festive feeling awakened by the Christmas bells is produced by cosmic causes active at this time of the year, and the present season is holy in very truth as we shall presently see. Those who study the stars know the signs of the zodiac as a cosmic sounding board, each sign vibrant with a particular quality; and as the marching orbs travel in kaleidoscopic procession from sign to sign in ever varying combination, the chords of cosmic harmony known to mystics as the "song of the spheres" sound a never ending anthem of prayer and praise to the Creator. This is not a fanciful idea but an actual fact patent to the seer, and capable of demonstration to thinkers by its effects. And the harmony of the spheres is not a monotone; it varies from day to day and from month to month as sun and planets pass from sign to sign in their orbits. There are also yearly epochal variations due to precession of the equinoxes. Thus there is infinite variety in the song of the spheres, as indeed there must be, for this constant change of spiritual vibration is the basis of spiritual and physical evolution. Were it to cease even an instant, Cosmos would be resolved to Chaos.

For demonstration, observe the nature and quality of the love life poured through the Christ-star, the sun, when it transits the belligerent sign of Aries, the Ram, in spring, Sex love is the keynote of nature; all its energies are applied in generation; then the passional propensities run riot. Compare this with the effect of the sun during December when it is focused through the benevolent Sagittarius, ruled by the planet Jupiter. Its ray is then conducive to religion and philanthropy; the air is vibrant with generosity, and the love life of the Christ-star find its highest expression through this congenial sign. Outwardly reigns the gloom of winter, for the visible symbol of "The Light of the World" has been onscured; but on the darkest night of the year Christmas chimes evoke a ready response to the Christmas feeling which makes the whole world akin, children of our Father in Heaven.

May the mystic music of the Christmas chimes awaken the tenderest chord in your heart, and may the keynote of joy be uppermost in your being during the coming year--this is the Christmas wish of the workers on Mt. Ecclesia.

SERVICE TO OTHERS DURING THE NEW YEAR

IT is cold in the Northern Hemisphere--old Boreas holds land and sea in his icy grip--but at no other time of the year are the hearts of men so warm. "A merry Christmas" and "A happy New Year" are salutations and expressions of good will which greet us everywhere. To most people they are only a breath flung to the breeze, but nevertheless they leave an atmosphere of kindness which is more important than is usually realized. The world would be richer if such cordial greetings were common all the year instead of being confined to this season. But, "if wishes were horse, beggars would ride" says the proverb; and unless our acts are directed towards the realization of our wishes, the benefit is nil. A certain sulphuric region is said to be paved with good intentions such as "well-meaning men" cherish, but the world needs works more than wishes.

Last month I asked you to join me in prayer for the efficiency of the Rosicrucian Fellowship in uplifting the world, and many letters have been received assuring me that the workers at Headquarters have the constant prayers of students. We know the power of prayer; without that grateful support we could never have endured the physical and mental strain incident to our phenomenal growth. But a few thousands are only as drops in a bucket compared to the millions who are seeking the light.

Christ said; 'LET HIM WHO WOULD BE THE GREATEST AMONG YOU BE THE SERVANT OF ALL." The worth of a man is measured by his services to the community. The same is true of an association; but, being a composite body, its efficiency as a whole depends upon the interest and enthusiasm of individual members. We are all under obligation to the Elder Brothers for the light we have received. It is our sacred duty to let that light shine so that others may share our great privilege (not disregarding others duties), and I therefore solicit your personal aid in making a systematic campaign to promulgate the Rosicrucian teachings more widely during the coming year.

This campaign should be carried on with discretion however. Let us beware of disturbing those of contented mind, but if you know of any one seeking for a solution to the Mystery of Life, please send us his or her name and we will send literature. Your name will not be mentioned unless you give permission.

We shall also be pleased to furnish you slips with information about the Rosicrucian Fellowship, as printed on the back of our postcards, if you will write for them. In this way you may interest your friends and open the way for further inquiry, and thus between us we may succeed in bringing the seeker LIGHT to his everlasting benefit. In helping your brother in his growth you are also helping yourself.

May spiritual prosperity and abundance of soul growth mark every day of your New Year.

SIEGFRIED, THE TRUTH SEEKER

AS we give our children picture books to convey moral lessons which they could not grasp intellectually, so the Divine Leaders of infant humanity used myths to convey great spiritual truths which have germinated for ages unconsciously to us, but have nevertheless been potent factors in shaping the line of human progress. You would scarcely thing that the Faust myth embodies the great problem of Freemasonry and Catholicism, and shows its ultimate solution, but we shall see in future lessons that this is true. At the present time I take just a point from the great northern epic, THE RING OF THE BIEBELUNG, to show how the great truth that the truth seeker must "leave father and mother," as Jesus and Hiram Abiff did, was conveyed to the Children of the Mist (NIEBEL is mist and UNGEN is children in German), who lived in the foggy atmosphere of Atlantis. Later I may take that legend up for consideration.

Wotan is the chief of the gods, who are always at war with the giants. They build a fortress called Valhalla where the Valkyries, daughters of Wotan, bring the faithful who have fallen in battle defending the faith. Truth lost its universal aspect when its warders walled it in and limited it. But Wotan has other children who love truth so dearly that they flee from Valhalla to be free. They are armed with a sword called "child of distress" (representing the COURAGE OF DESPAIR), wherewith the rebel against creed and dogma ever arms himself, casts conventionality to the wind, and seeks truth. Wotan sends his minions after the fugitives, and bids Brunhild the Valkyrie, who represents the SPIRIT OF TRUTH, to help slay them. She refuses; and Wotan, who has made himself invisible, parries the sword thrusts of his valiant son, Siegmund, who is killed in the unequal fight.

The dominant church does not view the complacence the secession of its children. It would even prostitute the Spirit of Truth to do its bidding, and when that fails, it uses subtle means to accomplish its ends. Its intentions were good, but it has degenerated. As Wotan puts Brunhilde from him in tears to sleep on a fire-girt rock, he tells her that she shall not wake till one appears MORE FREE THAN HE HIMSELF. Truth cannot be found in creed-bound religion; who seeks it must be untrammeled by allegiance to any one.

Such is Siegfried (translated, he who through victory gains peace), the son of the slain Siegmund and his sister-wife Sieglinda. The latter died after giving birth to him. He is thus free from father, mother, and all earthly ties; his only heirloom is a broken sword, the "Child of Distress." Fostered among the Niebelungen (ordinary mankind), he feels his divinity, and chafes at the limitations of his sphere. His foster father, Mimir, is a cunning smith; but every sword forged by him is shattered by the young giant at the first blow. Oft had Mimir tried to forge the "Child of Distress, and failed; for NO COWARD can do that. So long as we fear the church, public opinion, or anything else, we cannot free ourselves.

The courage of despair overcomes fear, and Siegfried finally forges the sword himself. With it he slays Fafner, the dragon of desire which broods over the treasures of the earth, and Mimir, his foster father, the lower nature. He is then absolutely free. A bird, the voice of intuition, tells him of Brunhilde, the beautiful Spirit of Truth, who may be awakened by ONE WHO IS FEARLESS AND FREE. Siegfried follows the bird of intuition on his quest; but Wotan, his ancestor, seeks to bar him with his spear, representing the power of creed upon which the sword in Siegfried's hand was once broken. That sword is stronger since Siegfried forged it, and Wotan's spear is weaker since the first blow, for creed always weakens when assailed. Siegfried, the free and fearless one, shatters Wotan's spear; and pursuing his way through the fire to the rock of the Valkyrie, he enfolds the beautiful Spirit of Truth in a loving embrace and wakens her with a kiss.

Thus the ancient myth told the truth seeker what was required to find truth. We must leave father and mother, creed, dogma, conventionalities, preconceived opinions, and worldly desires behind; we must never fear conflict with established authorities, but we must follow the inner voice through fire if need be; then, and then only, can we find truth.

Therefore the Rosicrucians insist that all who come to them for deeper teachings MUST BE FREE from allegiance to any school, and the candidate is not bound by oaths at any stage. Whatever promises he makes are made to himself, for liberty is the most precious possession of the soul, and there is no greater crime than to fetter a fellow-being in any manner. May we all remain true to the great heritage, and valiantly resists any infringement of this sacred right.

THE INCORPORATION AND FUTURE PLANS OF THE FELLOWSHIP

THIS month I have several important announcements to make and will use the monthly letter for that purpose. You remember that last year, in the series of lessons entitled "Our Work in the World," I spoke of incorporating the Rosicrucian Fellowship and placing the direction of its affairs in charge of trustees, so that that which belongs to the work may be preserved for its altruistic purposes during the centuries to come. Such an incorporation has now been perfected under the laws of California and the Fellowship has legal standing in the world. The Headquarter's site with the buildings now upon it, and the appliances necessary to carry on the work, are now the property of the Fellowship as a whole, safe from individual greed.

This has lifted a great load off the shoulders of Mrs. Heindel and myself. We have accumulated the contributions to the Fellowship, varying from a postage stamp to modest sums of money (for there have been no large amounts given as yet). With these small means carefully expended there exists now the foundation of something so immeasurably great that it is beyond my power of description. You, with your freewill offerings, have helped to create Mt. Ecclesia from the material point of view; yours it is and yours it shall remain, for neither Mrs. Heindel not I care for money or property, but glory only in the inestimable privilege of being of service. Much more is needed of course, so that the work may fully flower, but we rest our faith in the assurance of the Elder Brothers that when we are ready the things which make for greater growth and greater usefulness of the Rosicrucian Fellowship will come to us. Meanwhile we shall keep on laboring from day to day with the means already at our command; for thus, and thus only, can we fit ourselves for greater service.

It is also a great pleasure to announce that whereas we were before unable to obtain help, we have now several loyal co-workers at Headquarters; but though our office force has doubled within the last few months, so also has the work increased at a most phenomenal rate, and the rush in the office is as great as ever.

As you will remember, our earliest literature took notice of the fact that Science, Art, and Religion had been divorced in modern times, as separation was necessary to the thorough development of each. It was also stated that as Science, Art, and Religion were taught unitedly in the ancient Mystery Temples, so also must a union take place in the future for that is necessary to our spiritual growth. In June we shall start a School on Mt. Ecclesia to give out this composite teaching, with particular emphasis upon the art of healing. Prospectus and further particulars will be mailed to interested students upon application to Headquarters. The expenses will be met by offerings from those who attend.

FREE MASONRY, CO-MASONRY, AND CATHOLICISM

AT the end of last month's lesson a few words were said about men and women practicing Mystic Masonry, and it might appear to some as if we endorse Co-Masonry, but this is emphatically not the case. While we do not upon principle seek disparagingly of any legitimate movement, we have always warned our students against the Eastern religion as dangerous to the Wester world, though perfectly suited to the East. Co-Masonry is the outgrowth of a society promulgating Hinduism. In the winter of 1899-1900, the present leader of that society was in Rome, and one of her lieutenants accidentally found the Masonic rites in the Vatican library. These she copied without permission, and gave them to her superior, who took upon herself to write an extra degree. These are now the rites of Co-Masonry.

The foregoing statements are facts which we can prove; and we leave our students to form their own conclusions as the ethical efficiency and powers of soul-building possessed by a movement based upon rites obtained in such a manner. Besides, though we know positively that the rites came from Rome, we doubt that the abstractor eluded the vigilant watchers there. We believe that she unconsciously played into the hands of the Vatican. Thus Co-Masonry is both Hindu and Catholic in its origin. It is not recognized by the regular Masonic bodies, no matter what its founders claim.

In the closing lesson on Freemasonry and Catholicism we summed up the points concerning their cosmic relation in order to draw out the essence of the teaching; now for the closing word--the quintessence of our argument: The word "Freemason" is derived from the Egyptian PHREE MESSEN, "Children of Light." These words were originally used to designate builders of the Temple of God--the human soul.

Catholic means "universal," and was originally applied to differentiate the all-embracing World Religion--Christianity--from race religions like Hinduism.

The blood is the vehicle of the spirit; under the regime of Jehovah and the Lucifer spirits it became contaminated with egoism. Both Freemasonry and Catholicism aim to cleanse the blood and foster altruism.

Freemasonry teaches the candidate to work out his own salvation; Catholicism leaves him dependent on the blood of Jesus. Those who use the positive method naturally become the strongest souls; therefore Freemasonry should be fostered rather than Catholicism.

THE ROLE OF EVIL IN THE WORLD

IN last month's lesson we saw the value of discord in music; also the corresponding role of evil in the world, namely, to enhance by contrast the beauty and harmony of good. Thus it might seem at a superficial glance as if the apparent evil had been designed by God, the Author and Architect of our system--as if He were responsible for all the pain and sorrow under which the world is groaning. Such is not the case however. The Bible says truly that the Elohim, who were His agents, "saw that it was good" when their labor was done. Our ROSICRUCIAN COSMO-CONCEPTION and Lectures 13 and 14 explain in detail the Bible story of how the apparent evil came in through the Lucifer spirits; and that when it had entered, the forces which work for good used it to serve a beneficent purpose and to achieve a higher good than possible without this factor.

In the latter part of the Lemurian Epoch and in the early Atlantean times, man was pure and innocent--the docile ward of guardian angels who guided his every step upon the path of unfoldment. He had no reason; that would have been unnecessary when there was only one path to follow, for in that state there was no choice. The Lords of Venus were sent to foster goodness, love, and devotion. Had no disturbing factor entered, this earth would have remained in a paradise, and man would have been as beautiful flower therein. Pain, sorrow, and sickness would have been unknown. Under the regime of the lunar angels and the Lords of Venus, man would have grown wise and good automatically because there would have been no alternative. When the Lucifer spirits opened his eyes to the other course, and the Lords of Mercury fostered reason to guide him, he became potentially greater than either as required of those who follow the spiral path of evolution.

Thus equipped with choice and reason, it is man's glorious prerogative to elevate himself to the pinnacle of the greatest perfection possible in this scheme of evolution. Therefore Christ said: "He that believeth on me, the works that I do shall he do also; and GREATER WORKS that these shall be do." Let us learn from the Faust myth to follow in the footsteps of our preceptors by using the seeming evil to accomplish a greater good; let us learn not to be overcome by evil but to overcome it and transmute it into good. There is a saying that "whatever is, is best." If that were true there would be no incentive to strive for anything higher, better or greater. The words of the Savior urge us onward and legends like the Faust myth teach us how to use the seemingly destructive and subversive forces.

To whom much is given, of him much will be required. Students of the Rosicrucian Fellowship who receive the advanced Western Wisdom Teachings are particularly obligated to make great efforts. May we strive with all our strength to live up to our grand privilege.

P.S. Many new students have been added to our list since we asked your daily prayers for the workers at Headquarters. We therefore feel that it will serve a good purpose to reiterate the request to please include us in your devotions and ask that the Rosicrucian Fellowship Headquarters may become a most efficient Spiritual Center. We are, as you know from the prospectus, now about to open the School of Healing, and in this important step we feel the need of the grace of God as never before. Please help us so that we may succeed.

CHRIST, AND HIS SECOND COMING

ONE of the cardinal points in this month's lesson, and one concerning which widespread misunderstanding exists, had to do with the coming of Christ, and the vehicle he will use. The Bible gives the teaching very clearly, and the Western Wisdom Teachings of the Rosicrucians is in full accord therewith; hence it differs radically from the current conception of this matter, both among the majority of Christians and those who unwittingly or otherwise put forth false Christs to deceive the unwary. It is therefore of vital importance that scholars of the Western School should understand this matter thoroughly, so we will reiterate briefly the cardinal points of the Rosicrucian teachings given in the ROSICRUCIAN COSMO-CONCEPTION and elsewhere.

Christ is the highest Initiate of the Sun Period; the earth was them made of desire stuff, and His densest body was formed of that material.

No one can form a vehicle of material which he has not learned to mold; hence the Christ Spirit worked with our humanity from without the earth, as group spirits guide animals, until Jesus relinquished his dense and vital bodies at the Baptism. The Christ Spirit then descended into these vehicles, and ministered physically to man until the dense body was destroyed on Golgotha, when he became the indwelling Earth Spirit. The vital body of Jesus was them laid aside to await Christ's second advent.

Christ warned against imitators, and the question arises, How may we know the false form the real? Paul gives us such definite information that if we only heed it we are absolutely safe from deception.

Paul says (1st Cor. 15:50) that "flesh and blood cannot inherit the Kingdom." He insists that this body will be changed to the likeliness of Christ's own vehicle (Phil, 3:21), and in 1st John, 3:2 we find the same testimony.

Thus it is plain that any one who comes in a physical body proclaiming himself Christ is either demented and an object of pity, or else he is an impostor meriting scorn and reprobation. Nor are we left uncertain regarding the nature of the vehicle in which we shall meet Christ and be like Him. In 1st Thes., 4:17 we are informed that we shall meet the Lord in the air. Therefore we must necessarily have a vehicle of finer texture than our present dense body. The transformation will require ages so far as the majority are concerned.

In 1st Thes. 5:23 Paul states than man's whole being consists of spirit, soul, and body. When we shed the dense body finally as Christ did, we shall function in a body called SOMA PSUCHICON (soul body) in 1st Cor. 15:44. This is the "vital body" in our literature, a vehicle made of ether, capable of levitation, and of the same nature as the body which Christ used after the Crucifixion. This vehicle is not subject to death in the same sense as our physical body, and it is eventually transmuted to spirit as taught in our literature and as required by 1st Cor. 15th chapter.

Thus the Western Wisdom Teaching is in perfect agreement with the Bible when it teaches most emphatically that Christ will never come again in the flesh (that would be retrogression for Him). As a larva bursts its imprisoning cocoon and is transformed into a butterfly which wings it way among the flowers, a gorgeous bit of animated beauty--so shall we some day shed this mortal coil which weights us down to earth, and cleave the sky as living souls radiant with glory, hastening to meet out Savior in the land of souls, the New Haven and the New Earth. This is one of the main doctrinal points of the Rosicrucian School, and we trust that our students will endeavor to thoroughly master the subject so that they may be able to "give a reason" for their faith.

THE VITAL BODY OF JESUS

LAST month's lesson brought out a number of points not heretofore taught in public. But other mysteries bearing upon the scope and limitation of spiritual powers, and on the preservation of the vital body of Jesus against attack of the black forces, are also involved in the conversation between Faust and Lucifer. When the latter begs that the five-pointed star be removed so that me may leave, Faust asks "Why through the window not withdraw?" People who study mysticism often have a highly exaggerated idea of the power vested in one who has evolved spiritual sight. As a matter of fact, occult investigators are limited by laws of nature appertaining to the invisible world, as men of science are forced to conform to laws of physics.

In order that balance may be maintained, the laws in one realm of nature sometimes act directly opposite to the laws in another. Here in the dense physical world forms gravitate toward the center of the earth. Did not the solidity of the dense body prevent, we could reach the Christ without effort. It requires power to lift a body even an inch above the surface of the earth; spirit forms, on the other hand, have a natural tendency to levitate. It is therefore comparatively easy for a master of the black art to go to Mars propelled by the sex power stolen from his victims. He is naturally attracted to the planet of passion, and as the aura of Mars intermingles with that of the earth the feat is far from difficult. But he cannot penetrate even the first of the nine layers of the earth which lead to the Lord of Love, who is the Spirit of our sphere. Such penetration is the Path of Initiation; it takes soul power, purity, and self-abnegation to reach Christ and that is the reason why so few have anything to say about the earth's inner constitution.

We do not see physical objects OUTSIDE the eye; they are reflected on the retina, and we see only their "image" INSIDE the eye. As light is the agent of reflection, objects which resist the passage of light appear "opaque"; other substances, like glass, seem clear because they admit light rays readily. When the spiritual sight is used, light of superlative intensity is generated INSIDE the body between the pituitary body and the pineal gland. It is focused "through" the so-called "blind" spot in the eye directly upon the object to be investigated. The scope of the direct ray is entirely different from the range of the reflected physical ray. It penetrates a wall without difficulty, but no spirit in the desire world can see through glass. Neither Lucifer nor any evil spirit ever dares to go through anything made of that material, even the thinnest windowpane.

Knowing these facts, our Elder Brothers have placed the vital body of Jesus in a sarcophagus of glass to protect it from the gaze of the curious or profane. They keep this receptacle in a cavern deep in the earth, where no uninitiated can penetrate. To make assurance doubly sure, however, vigilant watchers keep constant guard over their precious charge; for were that vehicle destroyed, Christ's only avenue of egress would be cut off, and He would have to remain a prisoner in the earth until the Cosmic Night dissolves its chemical elements into chaos. Thus the mission of Christ as Savior would have failed; His suffering would be greatly prolonged, and our evolution would be enormously retarded.

Let us work, watch, and pray for the glad day of His liberation.

IMPROVING OUR OPPORTUNITIES

ONE of the most important points brought out last month is the fact that we have power to lengthen our life materially by earnest application to the purpose of existence--acquisition of experience. Whether we know it or not, every act of our lives hastens the end, or defers it, in a measure dependent upon whether the act is in harmony with the law or not. If we do not apply ourselves to the labor of life, or if we persistently follow a path that is subversive of soul growth, our discordant life destroys the archetype.

Rebirth is an altered environment then gives us a chance to retrieve the neglected opportunities. On the other hand, when we live in harmony with the plan of life inscribed in the archetype of our dense body, there is a constructive consonance in their vibrations which lengthens the life of the archetype and, consequently, also the life of the physical body.

When we realize that our life on earth is the seed time, and that the value of our post-mortem existence is in direct ration to the increment we have earned on our talents, it will be at once apparent how supremely important it is that our faculties should be used in the right direction. While this law applies to all mankind, it is superlatively vital to aspiring souls; for when we work for Good with all our might and main, each added year of life increases our heavenly treasure enormously. Advancing years give greater skill in soul culture, and the fruit of the last few years may easily outweigh that acquired in the first part of the life.

If we feel that this is true, and if we are anxious to reach the highest degree of attainment, the question naturally presents itself, How many we know the right way? And the answer is not difficult; the stars tell the tale. They show our abilities and the time most propitious to sow the seeds of the soul, to help, and to heal. Therefore the Rosicrucian Fellowship places must stress upon the study of the stars. In the horoscope these matters are accurately foreshown. Knowledge of what it says is power, and this knowledge, the power that goes with it, and the resultant soul growth, are within reach of every one who will study the simplified system contained in our corresponding course in astrology. If you have not already started, and are anxious to progress, I would suggest that you send for application blank, begin at once so that you may learn how to use your life to the ultimate of progress.

While I am suggesting immediate steps towards attainment, it may be in season to call attention of students to the fact that when they have been six months (*) on the correspondence list as students, they become eligible to apply for admission to the Inner School; and though the esoteric lessons in healing issued to probationers contain only a faint outline of the teachings given at Headquarters, they are a very material aid to the aspiring soul.

On August 6th at 2:00 P.M., we are going to lay the foundation for the nucleus of our Sanitarium, so that we may commence forthwith to care for the sick and give our students practical experience. Please join us in prayer for the success of the work. More details will be given in the ECHOES which we shall publish on the 10th of each month in the future.

* The time is now two years.

A PLEA FOR PURITY

THE most important point in last month's lesson is the power of passion to degenerate those who indulge in it. This we illustrated in the case of apes, which have been held back and have degenerated into animal-like forms because of their action in abusing the creative force. The responsibility of the Lucifer spirits for that condition has been brought out in the COSMO-CONCEPTION, and also the fact that the apes may overtake us if they advance sufficiently before the middle of the next revolution.

But there is an added responsibility in knowledge, as Christ said: "For unto whom much is given of him shall be required." And while the transgression in those early days may be overlooked and entail only a retardation during millions of years, the condition of one who has the light of the greater knowledge given to humanity today, and who transgresses the law by abusing the creative force, may become far more serious than that of the class now embodied in the anthropoid forms.

Black Magic is practiced much more commonly than one would suppose, sometimes almost unconsciously, for the dividing line may often lie in the motive. If, however, we abuse our superior knowledge, though we may be more refined in the indulgence of our passions, the result is certain to be disastrous. At this present stage, the vital force (save the insignificant quantity required to propagate the race) should be transmuted into soul power. Let us, therefore, continue steadfastly upon the path of purity so that worse may not befall us than the fate which has met those degenerate humans found as wards of Lucifer in the witches' kitchen--as represented in the Faust myth.

If we are tempted at any time by unclean thoughts, let us at once turn our minds to another subject far removed from sensuality. Above all, let us respect the laws of our country which require the ceremonial of marriage prior to union; for though the words of the marriage ceremony do not mate people, it is, nevertheless, meet that we who profess high spiritual ideals should not offend the common decencies by living together without wedlock. Those above the law render perfect obedience as Christ did, for when we comply with all laws without rebellion because it is right to do so, then we have risen above the law and are no longer in bondage.

THE FAUST MYTH AND THE MASONIC LEGEND

LAST month's lesson finished our consideration of the Faust Myth; and, taking a review of it as a whole, we note that it brings out the same idea as the Masonic legend. On the one had we have Rosicrucian and Lucifer; on the other, Marguerite and the priests. Marguerite shows faith in the church even in the darkest hour. This faith is her comfort and stay, and eventually she attains to the goal of the spirit. She reaches her heavenly home by faith. Her sins of omission and commission are due to ignorance; but when she sees the evil power embodied in the character of Lucifer and is offered freedom from prison and death, she declines to flee in such company; thereby she has redeemed herself sufficiently to merit a place in the Kingdom. Likewise, the wards of the church, the Sons of Seth, are today depending upon the atonement rather than upon their own deeds. They are looking for salvation through faith as their power of works is but small.

In Lucifer and Faust we find replicas of the Sons of Cain, who are positive, strong, and active in the world's work. The same spirit which imbued Cain with a desire to make "two blades of grass grow where formerly there was but one"--the independent, divine creative instinct which has caused the Sons of Cain in all ages to carry on the world's work--is also strong in Faust; and the glorious use to which he puts the powers of evil, namely, making them build a new land, a free one, where a happy and free people may dwell in peace and contentment, gives us a view of what the future has in store for us.

By our own works, by putting the evil powers to good use, we shall eventually free ourselves from the limitations of both church and state which now hold us in bondage. Through the conventions of society and the laws of the land are now necessary to restrain us from infringing on the rights of others, there will come a day when the spirit will ensoul us and purify us as the love of Faust for Helen purified him and gave him the incentive to use the Lucifer forces in the manner indicated. When we have conquered the desire to work for self, when we become enamored of our work for others as Faust was when with his dying vision he gazed upon the land that was rising from the sea, then we shall never require the restraining feature of the laws and conventions for we shall have risen above them by compliance with the every requirement. Only in that manner can we become really free. It but very difficult to enforce obedience on ourselves even though we may intellectually assent to the mandates of conventionality. As Goethe says:

"From every power that holds the world in chains,
Man frees himself when self-control he gains."

The Faust myth tells us there is such a utopian state in store for us when we have worked out our salvation by using the titanic forces within to make us really free. May we all strive by our daily actions to hasten that day.

EASTERN AND WESTERN METHODS OF DEVELOPMENT

WE receive frequent requests for help from people who unfortunately have belonged to societies where they came under the domination of spirit controls who now haunt and hound them until life becomes a burden. We also receive requests for help from people who have frequented societies teaching the Hindu breathing exercises. The impatience to enter the invisible worlds prompts many such people to take up exercises, the dangerous nature of which they do not realize until it is too late and they are broken down in health and spirit. They they come to us asking for a relief which we have unfortunately been able to give to all who have so far applied, even though some were on the verge of insanity.

Therefore the Rosicrucian literature has been replete with warnings to shun all Eastern breathing exercises, as they are unfit for Western people. It is with considerable sorrow that we have heard of a student who is now ill as a consequence of breathing exercises. We therefore feel that it may be well to once more state the reason for the difference between the Eastern and Western methods so that it may be made clear why it is wise to refrain from such exercises.

In the first place, it is necessary to realize that the evolution of spirit and the evolution of matter go hand in hand. The spirit evolves by dwelling in vehicles of dense matter and by working with the material found in the world. Thus, the spirit progresses, and matter is also being refined because the spirit works with it. The more advanced spirits naturally draw to themselves finer matter than those behind them upon the path of evolution, and the atoms in the bodies of a highly evolved race are more sensitive than those of the earlier peoples.

Therefore the atoms of cultured people in the West respond to vibratory waves not yet contacted by those who dwell in Eastern bodies. Breathing exercises are used to awaken the sleeping atoms of the Easter aspirant, and a vigorous course of this treatment is necessary to raise his vibratory pitch. The American Indian or Bushman might take these exercises with impunity for years, but it is an entirely different matter when a person with a highly sensitized Western body attempts such treatment. The atoms of his or her body have already been sensitized by the ordinary evolution; and when the person receives the added impetus of breathing exercises, the atoms simply run riot, and it is extremely difficult to bring them into proper repose again.

As it may do some good it may not be amiss to mention that the writer had had personal experience in the matter. Years ago, when he started on the Path and was imbued with the characteristic impatience common to ardent seekers after knowledge, he read of the breathing exercises published by Swami Vivekananda and commenced to follow directions with the result that after two days the vital body had been pulled out of the physical. This produced a sensation of walking on air, of being unable to get the feet down on solid ground; the whole body seemed to be vibrating at an enormous pitch. Common sense then came to the rescue. The exercises were stopped, but it was fully two weeks before the normal condition of walking on the ground with a firm step was experienced, and before the abnormal vibrations ceased.

In the parable, it is said that some were thrown out who had no wedding garment. Unless we first evolve the soul body, any attempt to enter the invisible worlds spells certain disaster; and any teacher who professes ability to railroad people into the invisible realms is not to be depended upon. There is only one way--patient persistence in well-doing.

THE REASON FOR THE MANY DIFFERENT CULTS

THE central through in last month's lesson, and one that we should ponder well is the reason why there are so many different cults. each with its own creed and with the idea that it alone has the truth. The reason for this condition, as shown in the lesson, lies in the fact that the ego has limited itself by entering into a vehicle which separates it from every one else. Because of this limitation, it is incapable of appreciating absolute and universal truth; and, consequently, religions teaching only partial truth had to be given.

The warfare and strife engendered in the world by the segregating influences of creed are not without their benefit either, for were all of the same opinion regarding the great question, "What is truth?" there would be no deep search for light or knowledge; and truth would not leave the strong impression upon us which we gain by the fight for that which we believe. On the other hand, the militancy of the churches shows to those who, as pioneers, are now taking a broader view--who recognize that none have more than a ray of the whole truth at present and who look to the future for enlargement of the cup of their capacity--that sometime they shall no longer see through a glass darkly, but shall know even as they are known.

Knowing that there is a cosmic reason for creed, we should neither seek or force advanced ideas upon those who are as yet limited by the spirit of convention, nor imitate the militant missionary spirit of the churches, but, as the Bible says, give our pearls of knowledge only to those who are tired of feeding on the husks and who long for the true bread of life.

Discourse upon subjects related to this higher knowledge may help those who are aroused from the spiritual lethargy unfortunately so common in our day and age. But argument will never do any good, for those who are in an augmentative mood are not convinced by anything we may say. The realization of truth, which is alone potent to break down the barriers of limitation that engender creed, must come from within and not from without.

Therefore, though we should always be ready to answer the questions of those who wish to know, and be ready to give the reason for our faith, we should also be on our guard so that we may not force our opinion upon others; that, having escaped one fetter, we may not be bound by another, for liberty is the most precious heritage of the soul. Hence the Elder Brothers in the Western World will not accept a pupil who is not free from all other bonds, and they take care that he does not obligate himself to them or any one else. Thus alone can the ring of the Niebelung and the ring of the gods be dissolved. May we all strive to live up to this ideal of absolute liberty, at the same time, of course, taking care not to infringe upon the rights of others.

WHAT THE PUPIL MAY EXPECT OF THE TEACHER

CHRIST said, "By their fruits ye shall know them." Suppose that weeds were endowed with speech, Would we believe their claims if they professed to be grape vines? Indeed not, we would look for the fruit. And unless they were able to produce, their protestations--no matter how vociferously made--would make no impression. We are thus sufficiently wise in material matters to guard against deception; then why not apply the same principle to other departments of life? Why not use ordinary common sense? If we did, no one could impose on us in spiritual matters, for every realm in nature is governed by natural law, and analogy is the master key to all mysteries and a protection against deception.

The Bible teaches us very, very clearly that we should try the spirits and judge them accordingly. If we do this, we shall never be deceived by self-styled teachers; and we shall save ourselves, our relatives, and the Fellowship we love much sorrow and anxiety.

Let us, therefore, analyze the matter and see what we have the right to expect from one who lays claim to being a teacher. To do this we may first ask our selves, What is the purpose of existence in the material universe? And we may answer that question by saying that it is evolution of consciousness. During the Saturn Period, when we were mineral-like in our constitution, our consciousness was like that of the medium expelled from her body by spirit controls at materializing seance, where a large part of the ethers composing the vital body has been removed. The physical body is then in a very deep trance. In the Sun Period, when our constitution was plant-like, our consciousness was like that of dreamless sleep, where the desire body, mind, and spirit are outside, leaving the physical and vital bodies upon the bed. In the Moon Period, we had a picture consciousness like that which we have in dreams, where the desire body is only partially removed from the dense vehicle and the vital body. Here in the Earth Period our conscious ness has been enlarged to cover objects outside ourselves by placing all our vehicles in a concentric position, as is the case when we are awake.

During the Jupiter Period, the globes upon which we shall evolve will be located similarly to what they were in the Moon Period. And the INTERNAL picture consciousness which we then possessed will be EXTERNALIZED, as the Jupiter Period is on the ascending arc. Thus, instead of seeing the pictures inside ourselves, we shall be able, when speaking, to project them upon the consciousness of those we are addressing.

Now, therefore, when any one professes to be a Teacher, he must be able to substantiate his claim in that manner; for the true Teachers, the Elder Brothers, who are now preparing the conditions of evolution which are to obtain during the Jupiter Period, all have the consciousness pertaining to that period. Thus, it will be seen that they naturally and without effort use this external picture speech, and thereby at once given evidence of their identity. Only they are able to guide others with safety. Those who have not evolved to that point, even though they may be self-deceived, and through their intentions may be good, are unreliable and should not be trusted. This is an absolutely infallible gauge; and the claims of any one who cannot show this fruit are of no more value than the claims of the weed mentioned in our initial paragraph.

All of the Elder Brothers of the Rosicrucian Order possess this attribute; and I trust no one among our students will in the future allow himself or herself to be deceived into following exercises or going through ceremonies devised by any person who is not able to produce the fruit, and call up living pictures in the consciousness of those with whom he speaks.

WHERE SHALL WE SEEK TRUTH, AND HOW SHALL WE KNOW IT?

AT the close of last month's lesson we saw that Siegfried, the truth seeker, had arrived at the end of his quest. He had found the truth. Meditating upon the subject it occurred to me as profitable to devote this letter to a straightforward answer to the question: "Where shall we seek truth, and how shall we KNOW without doubt when we have found it" To be absolutely certain about this matter is of very great importance. For many who accidentally find their was into the Desire World, such as mediums for instance, are enmeshed in illusion and hallucination because of inability to know truth. Moreover, the Elder Brothers of the Rosicrucian Order give probationers a definite scientific teaching on this point; and in order to guard against the danger spoken of above, they make an actual test before admitting any one to discipleship. All must come up to a certain standard in this matter. It may, of course, surprise you that this discussion is not reserved for probationers or disciples, but the Rosicrucian Fellowship does not believe in secrecy or mystery. All who wish may qualify for any degree; and this qualification is not a matter of FORM but of living the life.

In regard to the first part of the question then, "Where shall we seek truth?" There is only one answer--WITHIN. It is absolutely a matter of moral development; and the promise of Christ that IF WE LIVE THE LIFE WE SHALL KNOW THE DOCTRINE is true in the most literal sense. You will never find truth by studying my own or any other books. So long as you run after outside teachers, myself or any one else, you are simply wasting energy. Books and teachers may arouse your interest, and urge you to live the life, but only in so far as you make their precepts a part of your inner self are you really seeking in the right direction. The Elder Brother--whom I, perhaps mistakenly, speak of as Teacher--has never taught me directly since the first short period when that which is embodied in the Cosmo was given. And in the last year I have learned not to ask question for I have noticed that whenever I did so he simply gave me a hint as to how I, myself, might obtain the desired information. Now, instead of asking questions, I ask for directions as to how I may solve a problem. So you see that it is by using our own faculties, which may be compared to he talents spoken of by Christ, that we get the information of most value to ourselves.

The second part of the question, "How may we know the truth?" is best answered by referring the student to the evening exercise given in the Lecture No. 11, SPIRITUAL SIGHT AND INSIGHT. It may be performed by any one regard less of whether he or she is a probationer of the Rosicrucian Fellowship or not. The teacher said at the time of giving it that if it were possible to prevail upon the most depraved person in the world to perform this exercise faithfully for six months, he would be permanently reformed; and those who are faithful have found that it sharpens all mental faculties, particularly the memory. Besides, by this impartial judgment of oneself night after night, one learns to discern truth from error in a degree not attainable in any other way. Not all our students may feel inclined to take up probationership, and we never urge any one to do anything in the Western Wisdom School. But if you really want to know the truth I can honestly recommend this method. It develops an inner faculty and no matter what statement is made to you, once you have developed this, you will know at once whether it rings true or the reverse.

WHY THE TRUTH SEEKER MUST LIVE IN THE WORLD

AFTER the transfiguration scene, when the Christ and His disciples were making ready to descend from the Mount, the latter would fain have stayed and suggested making dwelling places so that they might remain. This was not permitted, however, for there was work to do in the world which would have remained undone had their plan been carried out.

The Mount of Transfiguration is the "Rock of Truth," where the freed spirit may behold the eternal realities. There is the GREAT NOW (the past symbolized by Moses and Elijah) the prophets of the ancient dispensation met Christ, the ruler of the Kingdom which was to come. Every spirit who is permitted to behold the supernal splendors of this celestial realm, to hear the sublime strains of the harmony of the spheres, and to view the wonderful colorplay which accompanies the music, is likewise loath to leave. Were it not that we seem to lose our form and personality, and encompass this whole realm within ourselves, we should probably not have the strength to return to earth, but this feeling that we retain "heaven within" fortifies us when it is time to again turn our gaze outwards and attend to the work in the world.

Objects in the physical world always hide their inward nature or construction; we see only the surface. In the Desire World we see objects outside ourselves, inside and out, but they tell nothing of themselves or the life that ensouls them. In the Archetypal Region there seems to be no circumference, but wherever we direct our attention, there is the center of all, and our consciousness is at once filled with knowledge concerning the being or thing at which we are looking. It is easier to catch in a phonograph the tone which comes to us from heaven than to set down the experiences we encounter in that realm, for there are no words adequate to express them; all wee can do is to try to live them.

But to live them, however imperfectly, we must be in the world; we have no right to remain secluded with the truth we have found. That is the great lesson taught when Siegfried leaves his beloved. He must not remain. Life is a constant flux; stagnation is the cardinal sin, for new experiences are the very life breath of progress. If we have found truth, it is our bounden duty to seek also a field where it may be of use. And according to our judgment in that matter, and the diligence wherewith we plant and water, will be our harvest.

This is a matter we should each carefully consider: "What sue am I making of the teachings I receive?" We may be off in the mountain in dreamland, though we live in a city, and as deaf to the cry for light which sounds in our very ears as if the seeker were thousands of miles away. Unless we give out BY OUR LIVES--which speak louder than words--the truth we have found, we incur a heavy responsibility, "for unto whom much is given, of him shall much be required." Let us remember that "Knowledge puffeth up, but love edifieth," and that SERVICE is the standard of TRUE GREATNESS.

A METHOD OF DISCERNING TRUTH FROM ITS IMITATION

IN the February letter we discussed the question: "Where shall we find truth, and how shall we know when we have found it." But there is no use in seeking truth, or in knowing truth when we have found it, unless we put it to practical use in our life--and it does not follow that we will do that merely because we find it. There are people, comparatively many, who scour the civilized world to find rare treasure of ancient art--pictures or coins. There are many who manufacture imitations of the genuine articles, so the seeker after these things runs the risk of being duped by clever rogues unless he has means of knowing the genuine from the spurious.

In this respect he is beset by the same danger as the truth seeker, for there are many pseudo-cults and clever inventions that may baffle us. The collector often shuts his find up in a musty room and gloats over it in solitude; and not infrequently after years, or maybe when he has died, it is found that some of the things he guarded most jealously and treasured most highly were spurious and imitations of no value. Similarly, one who finds what he believes to be truth may "bury his treasure" in his own breast, or "put his light under a bushel," to find, maybe after many years, that he had been swindled by an imitation. Thus, there is need of an infallible final test, one which eliminates all possibility of deception, and the question is how to discover and apply it.

The answer is as simple as the method is efficient. When we ask how collectors discover that a certain article they prize is an imitation, we shall find that it is usually by showing it to some one who has seen the original. We may deceive all of the people part of the time and a part of the people all of the time, but it is impossible to deceive all the people all of the time; and had the collector shown his find publicly instead of hoarding it in secret, he would have quickly learned by the collective knowledge of all the world whether his find was genuine or not.

Now mark this, for it is very important: Just as surely as the general secretiveness of collectors aids, abets, and fosters fraud on the part of the curio dealers, so also the desire to have and to hold for oneself great secrets not known to the "rabble" fosters the busines of those who trade in "occult initiations" with elaborate ceremonial to beguile victims into parting with their cash.

How can we test the worth of an axe but by using it and thus finding out whether it will keep its edge in actual wearing work? Would we buy it if the salesman required us to put it in a dark corner where no one could see it, and forbade us to use it? Certainly not! We would want to use it in our work, and there it would show whether it had "temper." If it were found "true steel," we would prize it; if not, we would tell the salesman to take back his worthless stuff.

On the same principle, what is the sense in "buying" the wares of secrecy mongers? If their wares were "true steel," there would be no need of secrecy, and unless we can use them in our daily lives, they are of no value. Neither is a good axe of value to us unless we use it; it rusts and loses its edge. So it is obligatory on every one who finds truth to use it in the world's work, both as a safeguard to himself to make sure that it will stand the grant test, and to give others a chance to share the treasure which he himself finds helpful. Therefore it is very vital that we follow the command of Christ: "Let your light shine."

OUR RESPONSIBILITY IN GIVING OUT TRUTH

IN regard to last month's letter one of the students writes: "in your letter it would seem to be implied that there is no secrecy or discretion on the part of the individual who knows occult things, to be exercised in giving them out, and no personal responsibility incurred; at least your meaning does not seem to be made plain." It is, of course, impossible to cover a subject of this magnitude in a letter or several letters. But the question about the responsibility of giving out truth does really concern us in so far as the danger of misuse goes. My correspondent also says that "there are certain sects in this country which have certain powers that they use for selfish and avaricious purposes," and asks whether it would be wrong to withhold occult powers from them. Certainly not. But the Elder Brothers take care of that, and they are the real custodians of anything that is highly dangerous. Hypnotism, of course, is dangerous, but not to such an extent as the occult powers about which our correspondent asks.

During the ancient Israelitic dispensation darkness reigned in the Holy of Holies, and it was only permitted a few priests and Levites to enter the Temple. The High Priest alone was admitted into the Holy of Holies once a year. But at the Crucifixion the veil was rent, the Temple was flooded with light, and since then no secrecy has prevailed in Initiation. Yet it is in a certain sense as secret as ever, for as I said in last month's letter, it does not consist in ceremony at all. It is an inward experience, and we must have the power within ourselves to live that experience before it can come to us. It is secret in the same sense that the mysteries of square root are a secret to the child. No initiation fee could convey an understanding to the childish mind of the subject; he must live through a number of years and gradually mature to a point where it will be possible to enlighten him. When that point is reached, there is no difficulty about enlightenment. He will understand and see truth very readily.

It is exactly this truth of which I was speaking in last month's letter. The disciple must go through a period of training and by that training become mature and mellow to such an extent that he can live the truth within. Then when the time comes, it is very easy for the Teacher or Initiator to show him for the first time how to apply the trust which he has found, to use the power which he has stored up, and then he is initiated. But this experience cannot be told to anyone else. It is absolutely useless to try to convey it. It is not through ceremony or any other outward show that it comes to a man but as an actual result of his own past doing. Therefore he can apply its truth in his daily life, though others may be as absolutely unable to get at it as the child is incapable of appreciating what is happening when an example in square root is being done before its eyes. Thus are the real, vital truths guarded from all till the key of merit unlocks the treasure box.

WOMAN'S SUFFRAGE AND MORAL EQUALITY

FROM last month's lesson it will be evident, strange as it may seem, that the opera Tannhauser is the legendary plea for the much discussed woman's suffrage, which we hear so much of in modern times. It is evident also, as said last month, that like produces like; and a woman who is timid and afraid, who has been forced into marriage in a brutal manner, who feels herself owned, a chattel, not free to voice her ideas and ideals, cannot produce a noble, strong, and fearless offspring, one with the courage to adhere to its ideals. Therefore, so long as we hold woman in bondage, deny her rightful place in the world as the HELPMATE AND COMPANION of man, so long do we retard the race and our development. This is the esoteric reason why full equality must come about.

If men did but thoroughly realize and understand the idea that we are born in alternate embodiments, they would very soon accede to woman's just requests--if for no other reason than the selfish one that in their succeeding life they who are now men will take on the womanly garb, and have to live under the conditions which they are now making. Thus any man who is now holding back the just privileges from womankind will some day have to labor under these same conditions, while those who at present for which they are now contending without having to ask for them; but as the writer sees this matter, it is not exactly the privilege of voting so much as the moral equality which the woman feels she ought to have, and certainly she has a God-given right to that as well as man.

One point brought out in Tannhauser should particularly appeal to those who want to live the higher life, and that is that Tannhauser is held as strictly accountable before those of his friends who know of his crime as he is by the church. There is no double standard of morality in nature. Sin is sin by whomsoever it is committed, and more than that, to whom much is given of him much shall be required.

Therefore people who reach an enlightened stage must above all learn to live the clean and pure life in harmony with their professions. If, by enlightenment, we rise above the law, let us, as Paul says, not use our liberty as an occasion to gratify the flesh. The doctrine of "soul mates" and "affinities" has wrecked many a life which but for that would have been crowned with great soul growth.

What the shadow is to light, what "the devil" is to God--that is lust to love. Love is divine, a companionship of FREE souls. Lust is diabolical, and the transgressor a slave of sin, it matters not whether the outrage has been legalized by the state or blessed by the church.

Let us therefore strive to love each other after the spirit rather than after the flesh.

THE VICE OF SELFISHNESS AND THE POWER OF LOVE.

IN the last lesson we saw that the Lord of Wartburg asked the minstrel to describe love. As we all aspire to evolve within ourselves that quality, it is perhaps of very great importance that we should look the matter squarely in the face and see what is our greatest hindrance, for surely there can be no question but that we are all lacking woefully in respect to love. No matter what we may seem to others, when we look into our own hearts we stand ashamed, knowing the motives which prompted acts that others consider dictated by love of our fellow men. When we analyze these motives we shall find that they are all dictated by the one trait of selfishness; moreover, this is the one fault we never confess. I have heard men and women stand up publicly or in private and confess to every sin on the calendar save this single one of selfishness. Yes, we even deceive ourselves by imagining that we ourselves are not selfish. We see this trait of character very plainly in others if we are at all observant, but fail to perceive the beam in our own eye; and so long as we do not admit this great fault to ourselves and strive seriously to overcome it, we cannot progress upon the pathway of love.

Thomas a Kempis says: "I would rather feel compunction than know how to define it"; and we may well substitute the word love for compunction. If we could only feel love rather than be able to define it! But love cannot be known now by us except in the measure that we cleanse ourselves from the great sin of selfishness. Life is our most precious possession, and Christ therefore said, "Greater love (or unselfishness) hath no man than this, that a man lay down his life for his friends." In the measure, therefore, that we cultivate this virtue of unselfishness, we shall attain to love, for they are synonymous, as was shown by Paul in that inimitable thirteenth chapter of 1st Corinthians. When a poor brother knocks at our does, do we give him as little as we can? If so, we are selfish. Or do we help him only because our conscience will not allow us to let him go? Then also this is selfishness, for we do not want to feel the pangs of conscience. Even though we give our lives for a cause, is there not the thought that it is OUR work? Often I hide my face from myself in shame at that thought in connection with the

Fellowship, and yet we must go on. But let us not deceive ourselves; let us fight the demon of selfish ness and be ever watchful against its subtle onslaughts. If we find it whispering that we need rest and cannot afford to give our strength for others, or if we feel that we cannot afford to give our substance, let us force the virtue of generosity. As a matter of actual fact, we only keep what we give; our bodies decay and our possessions are left behind, but our good deeds remain ours for all eternity.

INITIATION NOT TO BE ATTAINED THROUGH BREATHING EXERCISES

IT is with considerable reluctance that I again take up the question of breathing exercises and their effects upon the body, but stern necessity compels me to sound anew the warning against the false and dangerous teachings which are promulgated by people who are either ignorant or unscrupulous in their desire for profit. Breathing exercises are absolutely contrary to the teachings of the Rosicrucian Fellowship, for under our teachings spiritual results may only be attained by spiritual methods and not by physical exercises. Unfortunately the great desire of students to attain quickly makes many an easy prey to such people. One of our very promising students is now in an insane asylum because he listened to the promises of a charlatan who offered to initiate him for the sum of twenty-five dollars.

I have just learned that in one of the Fellowship centers a man who has not been affiliated with Headquarters is charging various sums for horoscopes, contrary to our teachings. We annually return from Headquarters many dollars to people who send to us asking for delineations and character reading as well as predictions, because we uphold the principle that a spiritual science may not be prostituted for gold however much we need money; and it grieves us very much to find out that such people, who admit that they know these practices to be contrary to the principles of the Rosicrucian Fellowship, are placed upon the platform of study centers, and stand before the people as teachers an exponents, of the Rosicrucian teachings. This same person has also copied from Hindu books costing but a few cents, breathing exercises which he sells to unsuspecting victims for a dollar.

Now I ask you, dear friends, will you not take this from me, one who has gone the way and knows by experience that there is no express train to the Temple of Initiation. The road is slow and steep and rugged; it must be walked step by step, though th feet bleed, and the heart also with sorrow and suffering. The soul body--the golden wedding garment--which alone is the password by which we can enter, is made by the good deeds done day by day with patient perseverance in well-doing, and by no other method. Breathing exercises cannot take the place of good deeds. Can you not understand that? I know what I am talking about, because in the very earliest stage of my endeavor in spiritual directions, I also found these Hindu breathing exercises. I tried them for two days, and my vital body was partly lifted out of the physical; it then occurred to me that I was in a dangerous condition, and I stopped. But it took me two weeks to recover, during which I felt as if I could not get my feet on the ground, as if I were walking on air; and during those two weeks I suffered greatly. Others may not have the persistence to recover that I did, and may go to the insane asylum. Therefore it is a very dangerous thing to try. There may of course be others on whom they have no effect. But it is very, very dangerous to meddle with fire, and you should not try it. on the other hand, if you will day by day try to serve in the vineyard of Christ, and endeavor to do deeds of mercy, then the golden wedding garment, the soul body, will surely be woven, which one day will admit you to the Temple.

THE WORLD WAR AND INFANT MORTALITY

UP to the present time I have especially refrained from commenting upon current topics, but feel that the present cosmic crisis demands something from Headquarters which may guide students in their attitude towards this calamity. The effect of this unprecedented slaughter of human beings is much more far-reaching than is apparent from the physical viewpoint.

In the first place, of course, that viewpoint is the one which appeals to us. We feel and can sympathize with the grief felt in many thousands of homes, where father, son, or husband has been ruthlessly torn away. But the sorrow and suffering that are met with in the physical world fade into insignificance when compared with what takes place in the invisible realms of nature. The thousands and thousands of victims of this cruel war are awakening from the death stupor caused by the sudden transition from the physical life to that of the desire world. They carry with them the scenes of the battlefield; many are stunned and wander about in the most aimless fashion. They cannot realize what has happened. Others again are beginning to sense the fact that they have passed from one phase of existence to another. Then comes to them also the grief for those they have left behind. thus there is in the world at this time an indescribable, unimaginable amount of sorrow and suffering, mental as well as physical.

In fact, never since the world was has there been such universal sorrow as there is at the present time. But besides this, we must not forget we are now laying up for ourselves a great deal of future suffering; for, as has been explained in the Rosicrucian lecture literature, it is impossible for these people who are now so ruthlessly and suddenly torn away from their bodies to review their past life, and thus the etching of the life panorama does not take place as it should. Therefore these egos will not reap the fruit of their present existence as they should in purgatory and the first heaven. They will come back minus this experience at some future time; and it will be necessary, in order that they may regain what they have lost, to let them die in childhood so that they may have the new desire body and vital body imprinted with the essence of their present life.

Therefore in some far-off future day we shall find that an epidemic, or something of that nature, will take away many thousands of children, and we, now their contemporaries, will be left to mourn their loss. Oh! that this law of infant mortality were understood. Then we should not have to pray for peace as we are now doing. Let everyone in the Rosicrucian Fellowship pray morning, noon, and night for the restoration of peace at the earliest possible moment. Let us realize the responsibility of knowledge and live up to it, endeavoring daily to discharge it. This knowledge which we have received must be given out wherever it is practicable without intruding upon other people. If the world knew and believed in the law of rebirth and of consequence, if it understood the law of infant mortality, such a thing as this war could never have happened; and the more we try to inculcate these teachings, the better we shall promote peace and good will, and the better serve humanity.

Please be particularly earnest and concentrate every vestige of your power upon the healing work at Headquarters when we have healing meetings. We need all the help we can get.

THE INVISIBLE HELPERS AND THEIR WORK ON THE BATTLE FIELD

ANOTHER month has gone by and still the European war is raging in all its intensity. Thousands and thousands have passed over the border into the invisible realm, and the distress there as well as here is unprecedented in the history of the world. As you have learned from our literature, the desire world is the world of illusion and delusion; and those poor people who have so suddenly been transferred to that realm with frightful wounds upon their physical bodies also imagine (as very frequently in the case with persons who have met accidents) that the lesions of the physical body are still with them, and they suffer acutely there from these fancied injuries as they would here. That is of course entirely needless. many of them are going about there with dreadful wounds upon their bodies, particularly those who have wounds caused by bursting shells and by bayonets. It is of course an easy matter for the Invisible Helpers to show any one of these people that his or her injuries are only fancied, yet when there are so many thousands the task is gigantic, and our Invisible Helpers are having a time of unprecedented activity against overwhelming odds.

It is not so much however the anguish that results from such fancied bodily lesions which makes the work. The mental anguish--the concern for those who have been left behind, the fear of fathers concerning their little ones, and the sorrow of the mothers who have been left behind to bring up a family of young children--is the most fearful handicap to a settlement of this dreadful state of affairs that the Invisible Helpers have to meet, and this is the point on which I would like to ask your earnest co-operation.

President Wilson of the United States has appointed October 4th as a day of prayer for peace. It is well always to unite with such movements because our trained thoughts will have a considerable effect and strengthen wonderfully the general appeal. This day should be spent by every earnest student in prayer for the deliverance of the world from this awful slaughter. Their thoughts should be particularly directed towards soothing those who are in this world, and in the invisible world also who are distressed at the severance of family ties. Each one should hold the thought that although the present war seems grievous, nevertheless this is only an incident in a long stretch of time which has neither beginning nor end. As spirits we are immortal, and these things which now seem to us of so great importance, when viewed from the spiritual standpoint and when considering the fact that we are really immortal, are of less moment than now seems the case to us. Whatever befalls, it will be incorporated into the spiritual nature as a lesson to give us a sense of the horror of this carnage which is now devastating the world.

This war, let us fervently hope, will be the last war that will ever mar the peace of the earth; that having learned this costly lesson, mankind will once and for all destroy the implements of war, and beat their swords into plowshares. Let this idea be in the mind of every student on the 4th of October, but as this date is so near at hand that probably this letter will not reach all in time, let every one in the Rosicrucian Fellowship devote Sunday, the 18th, to a prayer for peace. By that time all our students will have received this message, and we shall again be united from morning until evening in this effort to help restore peace to the world. May the kingdom of Christ soon superseded the kingdom of men, for they have certainly shown themselves inefficient rulers.

THE WORLD WAR AND UNIVERSAL BROTHERHOOD

IN almost every mail we receive letters commenting upon the war, but with very few exceptions there has been no expression of partisanship, showing that the writers take a loftier viewpoint than inculcated by the various Race Spirits and commonly given the name of patriotism. This attitude is the only one consistent with the principles of the Rosicrucian Fellowship. We are all joined in an international association, we are all looking for the Kingdom which is to supersede all nations, and the fact that we were born on different parts of the globe and express ourselves in different tongues does not abrogate the command of Christ: "Thou shalt love thy neighbor as thyself," nor excuse us for playing the part of the "robber" rather than that of the "Samaritan." It behooves us in the Rosicrucian Fellowship to rise above the barriers of nationality and learn to say as did that much maligned man, Thomas Paine: "The world is my country, and to do good is my religion." We must cease to be merely national and strive to become universal in our sympathies.

But there is a war that is well worth fighting, a war upon which we may legitimately expend all our energy, a war that we shall do well to pursue with unrelenting zeal, and one of the students puts it so well that we cannot do better than give his letter.

"In reflecting upon the war this thought comes: When men grow weary of the appalling internecine struggle and lay down their arms, and peace holds sway, from this continent, burdened with the dust of friend and foe alike, its rivers running crimson with the best blood of empires, a new Europe will arise, and a higher civilization succeed the one destroyed.

"And the vast host of nameless dead, dying, will prove a mightier power for world peace than had they lived. Thus it is that from the unrestrained passions of men, Deity, just and loving, brings ultimate good.

"If men, and women too, were only one-tenth part as eager to wage war against their real enemy within the human breast as they are to take up arms against a supposed enemy just across a non-existing imaginary boundary line on the face of God's good world, then the Prince of Peace could come into His own. All deadly weapons would be consigned to limbo, and the glorious promise would be fulfilled: 'On earth peace and good will towards men.' "And so for myself, I resolve that i will not cease my efforts till the last vestige of evil, error, and hate be eliminated, and the lofty trinity of 'Goodness, Truth, and Love reign unchallenged within.' "In this real struggle I find myself a poor soldier, and the tide of battle often sets in the wrong direction, yet no matter if I fail ten thousand times, the lesson must be learned and shall be learned. Some day, with a stout heart, an indomitable will, and unflagging persistence, the victory will be won and peace will reign--the peace that passeth all understanding." let us all join our brother in that noble fight, remembering the words of Goethe: "From every power that holds the world in chains Man frees himself when self-control he gains."

DESIRE--A TWO-EDGED SWORD

THIS is the time when good wishes are in order. "A Merry Christmas and A Happy New Year" are greetings soon to be heard everywhere, and in conformity with this ancient usage the workers on Mt. Ecclesia also extend to members all over the world the usual seasonal greetings.

But while we thus cordially wish one another Godspeed and good cheer in the coming year, after all, though the wishes of others may be encouraging and gratifying, they are really of minor consequence. But what we wish ourselves individually is of prime importance. If the whole world conspired against and antagonized us in this wish, we should nevertheless succeed, provided always we were able to put sufficient intensity and insistence into the wish. Do we desire riches? They may be ours by the exercise of will. If we want power and popularity, they also are at our beck and call, provided we clothe our wish with an all-compelling ardor. Are we sick, feeble, or in other ways disabled? We may rid ourselves of these bodily ailments also by an intense desire for health. Social restrictions or hampering family conditions will disappear before the earnest desire of the one who wishes.

But there is another side. Desire is a two-edged sword, and what appeared the greatest good while in contemplation may prove to be a curse when we have achieved actual possession. The greatest fortune may crumble in a few hours by earthquake or a turn of the market, and the rich man always fears he may lose his possessions. To be popular we must be at everybody's beck and call; we have neither rest nor time to follow our own bent. Bodily ailments which seem thorns in the flesh, which seem to rob life of all its joys, and of which we would fain be rid, may be the greater blessing in disguise. paul had such an ailment and he besought the Lord, who said to him: "My grace is sufficient for thee." So also with inharmonious family conditions, etc. There are in all human relationships certain lessons to be learned for our good, and therefore we should be very careful not to wish them away without always adding the words which were used by Christ during the passion of the cross in the Garden of Gethsemane. Though in the body He shrank from the torture that awaited Him, He said: "Not my will but Thine.' We should always remember that there is only one thing we may pray for with unrestricted fervor and full intensity, and that is that we may be pleasing to God.

An now, dear friends, the Rosicrucian Fellowship is an association composed of many individual members. You are one, and will you join as a member in wishing ourselves, the Fellowship, a grater baptism of God's grace during the year 1915, so that we may more efficiently do our part of the work of God upon the earth and hasten the day of Christ? And will you wish it with such intensity that you will WORK for that end all through the year with zeal and fervor? May God bless the Rosicrucian Fellowship and make it a more efficient factor in His work in the world.

SPIRITUAL PROSPERITY FOR THE NEW YEAR

THE customary greeting at this time is: "May you have a happy and a prosperous New Year." With this the writer is in hearty accord and extends it to you, but his meaning may differ somewhat from that which is ordinarily given, for usually it is material prosperity that is the main thought; whereas the writer wishes you that gold which is wrought by the alchemy of the soul, so that the base metal of the coming year's experience may thus be transformed into the Philosopher's Stone, the greatest good this world can ever give. Worldly riches are always a source of care to their possessor, but this, the jewel of jewels, rings with it? the peace that passeth all understanding.

Moreover, if we work solely for material things, our labor is always found to be hard drudgery no matter how we may seek to break the monotony by indulging in so-called pleasures. There comes ever and anon the thought: "What is the use?" But when we labor in the vineyard of Christ, when we do everything in our business and out of it as "unto the Lord," then the aspect is entirely different. Christ said: "My yoke is easy, and my burden is light," and that is an actual truth, though perhaps not in the ordinary sense. The writer and others who have been with him during many years can testify from personal experience that though there has been the most arduous labor, both mental and physical, and though the body has been sometimes so tired that it has been almost impossible to bring it together in the morning, nevertheless there has been a satisfaction, joy, and pleasure that the world knows not, neither can understand. The years that have gone by, spent in this work, have been so satisfactory that nothing in the world could compensate the writer and his companion for them should they be lost. Year by year he estimates it a greater privilege to thus labor, and others who are with him have exactly the same feeling.

How about you, dear friend? We are at the beginning of a new year, a new start. The Rosicrucian Fellowship as an organization depends on the units, and if we are to make spiritual progress, then the burden must be taken up by every one among us. We must become more faithful, more earnest, more devoted to the ideals that have been given by the Elder Brothers. We know that there are faithful workers in the Fellowship, but are you? It is not enough to simply study the teachings and meditate upon them; we must actually carry them into our lives and because shining lights in our community. We must live the life not only in the outside world but right in the home, so that other members of the family may see the light and be brought in. We know that many do this, but there are others who are lukewarm, who still stand on the threshold and do not want to take the yoke. Now the yoke must be borne, no matter if the neck becomes calloused in the effort; in fact, every callous is an additional factor in building, the soul body, the glorious wedding garment in which alone we can meet the Lord when he appears.

It is the earnest, the very earnest hope of the writer that every student of the Rosicrucian Fellowship will take up his yoke with more ardor than ever before, so that both individually and collectively we may lay up treasure in heaven that is sure to be ours at the end of the year-day, when we have borne the burden and the heat.

LOVE, WISDOM, AND KNOWLEDGE

THIS month we are starting a new series of lesson on "The Web of Destiny-- How Made and Unmade," and we trust that this series will prove very profitable to you in your study and in your life. While the lesson are analytical and technical in some respects, the subject should be approached in a spirit of the deepest devotion by keeping the main purpose of life in view.

As you are probably aware, the word "philosophy" is composed of two words meaning love of wisdom. Most people have the idea that "love of wisdom" in this connection is synonymous with desire for knowledge, but as we have seen from a recent lesson, there is a vast difference between knowledge and wisdom. Wisdom implies love, first, last, and all the time, while knowledge may be used for the most evil purposes imaginable. In fact the true esotericist who is inspired by a fervent devotion in his study and his work in life is too modest to accept the title of philosopher, for to him it means even more as he turns it around and calls it "The Wisdom of Love" instead of love of wisdom. A little thought will very soon make the point clear. The subject we have chosen for the coming series of lessons is one of the most intimate and holy which one can take up, therefore you will readily realize that it must be approached in this "wisdom of love" spirit, in love that is embodied in the full realization of what true philosophy is and means.

Robert Burns once said:

"O wad some pow'r the giftie gie us
To see ourselves as ithers see us!"

But I am afraid that power would indeed be a sad possession though it may seem upon superficial thought to be desirable. Each of us is full of shortcomings. At times we make but a sorry figure on the stage of the world. Sometimes we seem to be thrown aimlessly hither and thither by the shuttlecock of destiny, while others who are unable to see the beam in their own eye are criticizing us and making us appear ridiculous. If we saw ourselves with their eyes, we should lose that most essential attribute--our self-respect; we should shrink from facing our fellow men.

When we realize that this is so (and thought upon the matter surely can not fail to convince us), then we might also with profit put the shoe on the other foot and realize that we ourselves, by sharp criticism of the trivial shortcomings of others, are taking a very unbrotherly, unphilosophical, un-wisdom-of-love-like attitude. It is the purpose of the coming lessons to give us an idea of what has caused in the past some of the things that we most criticize in others, so that we may be able personally to avoid similar mistakes; also that we may have that real, true, Christian charity which VAUNTETH NOT ITSELF, IS NOT PUFFED UP, SEEKETH NOT HER OWN, REJOICETH NOT IN EVIL BUT IN THE TRUTH, as paul describes it in that beautiful thirteen chapter of 1st Corinthians.

I trust that you will approach the lessons in that spirit and that they may be of lasting benefit to us all.

CONCENTRATION IN THE ROSICRUCIAN WORK

WHILE meditating upon the good of the Rosicrucian Fellowship the question came up before the writer's mind: "What is the greatest general hindrance to our progress in the spiritual work?" And the answer was: "Lack of concentration." We all have our families who crave and must have a certain share of our attention. Our work in the world must not be neglected on any account. We are here to accomplish certain things, and to learn by them. After these duties have been attended to there still remains for each of us a little time which we may justly and properly use for our own development, and it is as important that we properly use this extra time as it is that we attend to our worldly duties, our family, and our social obligations.

Consider now that in ordinary life we do not try to become a doctor and practice medicine today, work in a machine shop tomorrow, and every other day go at some other business. We know that such a course would not take us anywhere in life. neither do we live in one family as husband or wife today and assume similar relations in another family tomorrow; nor do we change our social circle as often as we change our coats or shoes. Such industrial and social conditions would be absolutely impossible. On the contrary, we pursue one line of work in the world; we look after one family; we concentrate our efforts in these departments of our life to the exclusion of all others.

Why not apply the same common sense to our spiritual endeavors? We study our business; we plan ahead; we work with all our might in order to make it a success. We also study the needs of our family and we plan for them. We know that success, both social and industrial, depends upon the amount of concentration and the amount of planning we do. If, then, we are so wise concerning worldly things, which last only for the few years of our earth life, can we not bring ourselves to use the same common sense to apply ourselves equally with all our mind and with our heart to the spiritual things that are everlasting? In the Atlantean Epoch when the Original Semites were called out from among their brothers, many of them accounted it a great hardship. They, "the Sons of God," married "the daughters of men," with the result which we know from our study of the COSMO.

We are today at another great parting of the ways. An "Ecclesia," or company of men, is being "called out" as pioneers of the next great race. Many roads lead to Rome and to the Kingdom of Christ, but if we fritter our time away walking on one today and tomorrow choosing another path, we are certain to fail; and I therefore urge all the students who are in sympathy with the ideas of the Rosicrucian Fellowship to give up all other religious societies and devote their whole heart, mind, and spirit to living and spreading our teachings.

Trained, skilled, and devoted workers are sought in our earthly enterprises. In the heavenly Kingdom loyalty and devotion also are prime factors.

Let us memorize and concentrate on the first three verses of the first Psalm, for surely we want to reap the greatest harvest that we possible can from our spiritual as well as from our material efforts.

THE COSMIC MEANING OF EASTER

AS this lesson will reach you about Easter time, I thought it might be well to devote the letter to that recurring event.

You know the analogy between man, who enters his vehicles in the daytime, lives in them and works through them, and at night is a free spirit, free from the fetters of the dense body--and the Christ Spirit dwelling in our earth a part of the year. We all know what a fetter and what a prison this body is, how we are hampered by disease and suffering, for there is not one of us who is always in perfect health so that he or she never feels a pang of pain, at least no one on the higher path.

It is similar with the Cosmic Christ, who turns His attention toward our little earth, focusing His consciousness in this planet in order that we may have life. He has to enliven this dead mass (which we have crystallized out of the sun) annually; and it is a fetter, a clog, and a prison to Him. Therefore it is right and proper that we should rejoice when He comes at Christmas time each year and is born anew into our world to help us leaven this dead lump wherewith we have encumbered ourselves. Our hearts at that time should turn to Him in gratitude for the sacrifice He makes for our sakes during the winter months, permeating this planet with His life to awaken it from its wintry sleep, in which it must remain were He not thus born into it to enliven it.

During the winter months He suffers agonies of torture, "groaning, travailing, and waiting for the day of liberation," which comes at the time that we speak of in the orthodox churches as the passion week. But we realize according to the mystic teachings that this week is just the culmination or crest wave of His suffering and that He is then rising out of His prison; that when the sun crosses the equator, He hangs upon the cross, and cries, "CONSUMMATION EST!"--"It has been accomplished!" That is to say, His work for that year has been accomplished. It is not a cry of agony but it is a cry of triumph, a shout of joy that the our of liberation has come, and that once more He can soar away a little while, free from the fettering clod of our planet.

Now, dear friend, the point to which I would like to call your attention is that we should rejoice with Him in that great, glorious, triumphal hour, the hour of liberation when He exclaims, "It has been accomplished!" Let us attune our hearts to this great cosmic event; let us rejoice with the Christ, our Savior, that the term of His annual sacrifice has once more been completed; and let us feel thankful from the very bottom of our hearts that He is now about to be freed from the earth's fetters; that the life where with He has now endued our planet is sufficient to carry us through the time till next Christmas.

I hope that this may furnish you with a point of view for prayerful Easter meditation which will result in abundant soul growth.

WASTE THROUGH SCATTERING ONE'S FORCES

IN the March letter I suggested, as you will remember, the concentration of energy in one direction, advising, as I have done before, that students devote all their spare time to work in and for one religious society, rather than scattering and dissipating their energies by member-ship in a number of such societies, for it is an impossibility to do effective work in that manner.

Since that time a few resignations have come in, which were not unexpected. Among a large membership like that of the Rosicrucian Fellowship some of those who hold membership in other bodies would naturally have their greatest sympathy somewhere else, and they would follow that bent in accordance with my advice. Indeed the surprise is that there have been only a few resignations, but this is no doubt due to the fact that Headquarters periodically weeds out those who show little interest, and thus keeps only the most live members on the list.

But the tone of these resignations does hurt. One writes: "I am a member of the Episcopalian Church; my pew rent is paid there, etc., etc." It seems strange that some will not understand that the Rosicrucian Fellowship is antagonistic to no church or society, particularly not to the Christian churches. It has been stated repeatedly that we favor membership in any Christian church. What the letter said was not CHURCHES, but "religious societies"; and, as said, it was not because we had anything against societies which work along Christian lines. There is, for instance the Unity Society of Kansas City, a clean, moral organization under a noble leadership, so far as we can learn from all reports. But to do one's best work in that or any other religious society one's entire energy in spare time should be given to that society alone; and if any member of the Rosicrucian Fellowship who is also a member of such an organization decides to cast his lot with them alone he is doing far better by them, far better by the Rosicrucian Fellowship also, than if he retains his membership in both. On the other hand, if the weight of his sympathies lies with the Rosicrucian Fellowship, then it is better for him, better for the Unity Society, better for the Rosicrucian Fellowship, that he cast his lot entirely with our association.

As we have often said, many roads lead to Rome, but you can not walk two roads at once. You must walk one in order to get there. Zigzagging from one to another is a waste of effort. If we do our work in the world we have but very little time left in which we may legitimately work for our own advantage along spiritual lines. Therefore we should endeavor to concentrate our efforts where they will do the greatest good instead of scattering our energies and attaining very little soul growth in that manner.

Moreover it should be understood that if at any time the policies of the Rosicrucian Fellowship do not meet with the approval of any one, he is not serving the cause by simply deserting the flag and railing against us from the outside. If he remains within we listen to him as one brother listens to another, and we see his arguments from a very different point of view than if he shows hostility, leaves, and becomes in that way an opponent. Then the same arguments would lose a good deal of their weight. We are all agreed about the great and cardinal points of our teachings. Every one of us surely appreciates the benefit that we have reaped from this philosophy which we are engaged in promulgating. Is it not meet then that we should be tolerant in matters of policy, that we may devote all our attention to the ideals?

EPIGENESIS AND FUTURE DESTINY

WHILE we are studying the "Web of Destiny--How Made and Unmade," it is expedient, in fact absolutely necessary, that we should keep before the eye of our mind the fact that life is not alone an unfoldment of causes set going in previous existences. The spirit, when it comes back to rebirth, has a varying amount of free will--according to the life previously led--to fill in details. Also, instead of only unfolding past causes into effects, there are also new causes generated at every turn by the spirit, which then act as seeds of experience in future lives. This is a very important point. It is a self-evident truth, for unless it were so, the causes that have already been set going must at some time come to an end, and that would mean cessation of existence.

Thus we are not absolutely forced to act in a certain way because we are in a certain environment and because our whole past experience has given us a trend toward a certain end. With the divine prerogative of free will, man has the power of Epigenesis or initiative, so that he may enter upon a new line at any time he wishes. He cannot at once steer himself out of the old life--this may require a long time, perhaps several lives--but gradually he works up to the ideal which he has once sown.

Therefore life advances not only by involution and evolution, but especially by Epigenesis. This sublime teaching of the Western Wisdom Religion of the Rosicrucians explains many mysteries not otherwise capable of a logical solution, among them one which has occasioned many letters to Headquarters. This subject is taken up with some reluctance as the writer dislikes speaking about the war. The question concerns the connection between a soldier, a woman of the enemy ravished by him, and the ego born of a mother who hates it because of the undesired motherhood.

Investigation of a number of cases has shown that this is a new venture on the part of the spirits coming to rebirth. All have been incorrigible in their previous environments and it seemed that no good could come by keeping them there to he sorrow of those with whom they were connected. The present war conditions, though not made for the purpose, afford an opportunity to transfer them to another field of action, where the new mother reaps, through this agency, the fruits of wrongs sown by herself in the past.

Nor is this condition at all peculiar to war. Very often similar means are used at other times so that we may reap what we have sown, through another soul who enters into our lives to suffer and to bring suffering to us. I have in mind a mother who told me a number of years ago how she rebelled against motherhood; how, after she had gone through the period of pregnancy with hate and anger in her heart, the little child was born and she refused even to look at it; but finally she was melted by pity for its condition of helplessness, and pity later turned to love. The child had all the advantages that money could give him, but these advantages could not save his mental balance, and today he sits in a murderer's cell in an asylum for the criminal insane, while the mother is left to sorrow and to ponder upon what she did or did not do during the time when that infant was coming to her.

Conversely, there are also occasions when a spirit, being through with an old environment, comes into a new sphere of action as a ray of sunshine and comfort to those who are fitted to receive that blessing by their previous actions. Let us, therefore, remember that no matter how degraded a being may be he has always the power to sow the seed of good, but must wait until that seed can flower in a right environment. Each of us, though bound by his yesterdays, is therefore thus far free respecting his tomorrows.

THE NEED OF SPREADING THE TEACHINGS

UPON re-reading the monthly lesson which accompanies this letter, embodying the result of investigations made some time ago, I was struck anew and with added force by the fact of the existence of such fearsome conditions about us. At the present time when the horrors of the great war are adding unprecedented numbers to those who pass from the present world to the invisible realms under harrowing conditions, it seems that an extra effort ought to be made to offset and to minimize the evil. The Rosicrucian Fellowship is as yet but a drop in the ocean of humanity, but if we do our share we shall earn a greater opportunity for service.

There is no remedy for the present conditions equal to a knowledge of the continuity of life and of the fact that we are reborn from time to time under the immutable Law of Consequence. If these great facts with all that they imply could be brought home to a large number of people, this leaven must ultimately work in such a manner as to change conditions all over the world. One man, Galileo, changed the viewpoint of the world concerning the solar system; and though we are only a few thousand, it is not possible for us to exert an influence upon the opinion of the world when we know that this is true? It is often said that people are not interested in spiritual matters; that you cannot get their ear; but, really, it is not so. Granting that of the hundred of thousands who went to hear Billy Sunday, the noted evangelist, a great many were actuated by curiosity or went to? jeer and sneer, there were also many thousand in whom was a strong desire for something which they themselves perhaps could not define, and which was the actuating motive. Recently there was a debate between a New York evangelist and a lawyer on the subject, "Where Are the Dead?" This debate was held in a large auditorium accommodating many thousands, and it lasted for three days. Every seat in the auditorium was taken and, if I remember right, there were many who could not even find standing room within. No, the world is seeking something; seeking it with a hungry heart, and it only depends upon us whether we are going to do our share by putting before the world the rational explanation of life which has come to us through the Elder Brothers. It is a great privilege and we should certainly take advantage of it.

But the question is, How? Let me ask you, would not YOUR newspaper take an occasional article on this subject? There are certainly a number of people within the Fellowship capable of writing such articles. A committee could be formed to receive the articles and furnish them to the members who ask for them and who would agree to take them to the editors of the newspapers in their respective towns and endeavor to get a hearing for the Rosicrucian Fellowship teachings through that medium. If an article is well written it is seldom refused when there is space available, for editors are only too glad to get something that they think may interest the reading public, even though they may not be in sympathy with it themselves.

Will some of the students who can write pleas submit short articles on "The Continuity of Life," and will those who are willing to undertake to get such articles into their home papers write and register their names to that we may get action? Address your communications in this matter to "The Publicity Department," Mt. Ecclesia.

I hope that this appeal will meet with a hearty response.

ASTROLOGY AS AN AID IN HEALING THE SICK

DID you ever realize the reason why Christ commanded that we should heal the sick? One of the reasons certainly was that when you have demonstrated that you can heal the body, those who have been helped will have more faith in your ability also to help the soul. When we have advanced to the high stature of Christ so that we can at once see the past and the present; when we are able thus to determine at a glance the causes, crises, and present stage of a disease, we shall need no other aid in diagnosis and advice. But until that time we must use such crutches as we have, and foremost among them is astrology.

Many people who have been unwilling to WORK for results have come to Headquarters expecting to gain spiritual illumination, to sprout wings, and to return to the world as wonder workers after a few days' stay. And naturally, they have been disappointed. But whenever anyone has honestly and earnestly applied himself to real work, not classes, for a reasonable time, results have always been attained. We have here a letter from a friend who stayed at Mt. Ecclesia and applied himself earnestly and honestly to his studies. We give his experience as encouragement to others to do likewise: "Dear Friends: The proposition which I expected to take up after my stay on Mt. Ecclesia turned out to be a graft on people and not consistent with our ideals at all, and I therefore sent in my resignation. No sooner, though, did I give up that scheme than I had an invitation from a prominent physician in Kansas City to do work with him. He appealed to me as being all right. We were literally stormed with patients. Mrs. Heindel, it is wonderful how people hunger for something of this nature; they look for someone to open their lives, and they try to get encouragement from sources that are more potent and reliable than the hard and dry life-destroying materialism.

"Astrology came as a wonderful help to me to gain their confidence; and by the aid of God, who sent me here, I was able to send them away, their ailments correctly diagnosed. And the strangest part of it is that none of them gave me any symptoms. I located both disease and symptom, and nearly everyone agree that I was right and resolved to live up to the high principles of manhood and womanhood which I enunciated to them.

"I expect to be very busy here and wish to thank you for the help I have received along this line during the last year at Mt. Ecclesia. I certainly enjoyed my stay with you immensely and am looking forward to a great deal of good from my work there; am only sorry I was unable to stay longer." What man has done, man can do. Mrs. Heindel and myself did not get our knowledge along this line without effort. We had to work hard for it; and others who have worked as hard with the same spiritual ideals in view, namely, the helping and uplifting of humanity, also find an illumination that is not given to those who are looking for the material rewards of life and their own aggrandizement. It seems to me that it is time the Rosicrucian Fellowship should wake up and take this study earnestly in hand so that healing centers may be established in every city in the world.

We have started a department in the magazine where we delineate the horoscope of children to help parents to know their latent characteristics. There is also a correspondence course for beginners, besides the course in Astro-Diagnosis and Astro-Therapy for probationers, and we would advise all who have not yet started to take up the study.

UNNATURAL MEANS OF ATTAINMENT

WHEN one investigates a certain subject in the invisible world, many fascinating byways open up, he is constantly lured away from the main line of research by this, that, or the other theme which attracts his attention, and there is great danger of losing sight of the goal and of wandering off in a maze of incoherency. Sometimes the temptation to follow a bypath is stronger than my power of resistance; and recently, while working on the "Web of Destiny," the figure of a hermit who had starved his body to the semblance of a skeleton--who had whipped himself till the blood flowed from sores that were never allowed to heal, and thought he was serving God by these austerities--led me to search for the origin of this hideous practice. I have written a lengthy article on the subject for our magazine; but as the matter is important, and many of the students are not subscribers to the magazine, I have deemed it best to give you the main facts.

In the ancient Mystery Temples the main truths now taught by the Rosicrucian Fellowship concerning the vital body were given to the aspirant to Initiation. He learned that this vehicle was composed of the four ethers: the Chemical Ether, which is necessary to assimilation; the Life Ether, which furthers growth and propagation; the Light Ether, which is the vehicle of sense perception; and the Reflecting Ether, which is the receptacle of memory.

The aspirant was thoroughly instructed in the functions of the two lower ethers as compared with the two higher. He knew that all the purely animal functions of the body depended upon the density of the two lower ethers and that the two upper ethers composed the soul body--the vehicle of service in the invisible world. He aspired to cultivate this glorious garment by self-abnegation, curbing the propensities of the lower nature by will power, just as we do today.

But some, who were overzealous to attain, no matter how, forgot that it is only by service and unselfishness that the golden wedding garment, composed of the two higher ethers, is grown. They thought the occult maxim, "Gold in the crucible, dross in the fire; light as the winds, higher and higher," meant only that so long as the dross of the lower nature was expelled, it did not matter how it was done. And they reasoned that as the Chemical Ether is the agent of assimilation, it could be eliminated from the vital body by starving the physical body. They also thought that as the Life Ether is the avenue of propagation, they could by living celibate lives starve it out. They would then only have the two higher ethers, or at least these would be much larger in volume than the two lower.

To that end they practiced all the austerities they could think of, fasting among others. By this unnatural process the body lost its health and became emaciated. The passional nature, which sought gratification by exercise of the propagative function, was stilled by castigation. It is true that in this horrible manner the lower nature seemed to be subjected; and it is also true that when the bodily functions were thus brought to a very low ebb, visions, or rather hallucinations, were the reward of these people; but true spirituality has never been attained by defiling or destroying "the temple of God," the body, and fasting may be as immoral as gluttony.

Let us endeavor to use moderation in all things, that we may be worthy examples to others and earn admission to the Temple by virtue of right living.

THE RACE SPIRITS AND THE NEW RACE

AS there are a great number of students who have not subscribed for the magazine, and as there is a very important article running now, dealing with the occult side of the war, i feel that it may be best to devote the monthly letter to a resume of the facts, and trust that this will also benefit those who take the magazine; for as I do not intend to copy, but will take up the subject offhand, new points are sure to be brought out.

You remember how every one of the countries concerned in this sad affair has endeavored to disclaim responsibility from the beginning. In a sense they are right, for though all have been guilty of pride of heart and, like David when he numbered Israel, have put their trust in the multitude of their men, ships, and armament, no war can ever take place that is not permitted by the Race Spirits. The Race Spirit guides its charges upon the path of evolution, and, like Jehovah, fights for them, or allows other nations to conquer them, as required to teach them the lesson needful for their advancement.

When seen by the spiritual vision the Race Spirit appears like a cloud brooding over a country, and it is breathed into the lungs of the people with every breath they take. In it they live, move, and have their being, as a matter of actual fact. Through this process they become imbued with that national fellow-feeling which we call "patriotism," which is so powerfully stirring in time of war that all feel wrought up about a certain matter and are ready to sacrifice all for their country.

America has no Race Spirit as yet. It is the melting pot wherein the various nations are being amalgamated to extract the seed for a new race; therefore it is impossible to arouse a universal sentiment which will make all move as one in any matter. This new race is beginning to appear, however. You may know them by their long arms and limbs, their lithe body, their long and somewhat narrow head, high crown, and almost rectangular forehead. In a few generations I expect they will be taken in charge by an Archangel, who will then begin to unite them. This itself will take generations, for though the pictures originally stamped in the old race bodies have faded from sight with the advent of the international marriages, they are still effective, and the family connections of America with Europe may be traced in the Memory of Nature found in the Reflecting Ether. Until this record has been wiped clean, the tie with the ancestral country is not entirely broken, and the colonies of Italians, Scots, Germans, English, etc., remaining in various part of this country retard the evolution of the new race. Probably the Aquarian Age will be here before this condition has been entirely overcome and the American race fully established.

If you look back at the developments during the past 60 or 70 years, it must be evident that it has been an age of skepticism, doubt, and criticism of religious subjects. The churches have become increasingly empty, and people have turned to the pursuit of pleasure, from the worship of God. This tendency was on the increas in Europe until the advent of this war, and it is still a disgrace to certain cities and centers of scientific thought in America. As a result of this worldwide attitude of mind, fostered by the Brothers of the Shadow with the permission of the Race Spirits, as Job was tempted by Satan in the legend, a spiritual cataract has covered the eyes of the Western world and must be removed before evolution can proceed. How that is being done will be the subject of the next letter.

THE WAR AN OPERATION FOR SPIRITUAL CATARACT

YOU are aware from the teachings of the COSMO that there was one race at the end of the Lemurian Epoch, there were seven in the Atlantean Epoch, seven in the Aryan, and there will be on in the coming Galilean Epoch, making in all sixteen races. You also remember that these sixteen races are called by the Elder Brothers "the sixteen paths to destruction" because enmeshed in the bodies of any race to such an extent that it will be unable to follow the others along the path of evolution. During the Periods and Epochs there is always plenty of time so that the Leaders of humanity can marshal their flocks into line. But the Jews are an example of what may happen to people who become so intensely imbued with the racial spirit that they absolutely refuse to let go. They continue as an anomaly among the rest of humanity, a people without a country, king, or any other of the factors that make for racial evolution.

This was the tendency among the nations of Europe up to the present war. Patriotism, and the racial ideal fostered thereby, were leading them away from God. An age of doubt and skepticism had been ushered in by the many scientific discoveries, and the pioneer races in the Western world were stearing very close to the brink of destruction. Therefore it became necessary for the Elder Brothers to devise measures whereby mankind might be brought from the path of pleasure to the path of devotion, and this could only be done by removing the spiritual cataract from a sufficiently large number of people so that they would then override the doubt and skepticism of the rest.

When we dwelt under the water in the early Atlantean Epoch, we were, as you know, unable to see the body or even to feel it, because our consciousness was focused in the spiritual realm. We saw one another, soul to soul. We were unaware of either birth or death, and we felt no separation from those we loved. But when we gradually became aware of our bodies, and our consciousness was focused in the physical world from birth to death, and in the spiritual world from death to birth, there was a separation, and consequent sorrow on account of the advent of death. In bygone ages however, there were still many who were able to see both worlds; they formed quite a considerable number of the populace. Their testimonies to the continuity of life were a great comfort to those who had been bereaved, for they believed thoroughly that those whom they had lost were still alive and happy, though unable to make themselves known. But gradually the world became more and more materialistic; faith in the reality of the hereafter faded, and sorrow at the loss of the loved ones grew more and more intense, until today many believe the separation is final. To them the word "rebirth" is an empty sound, and therefore grief is overwhelming.

But this very grief is nature's remedy for the spiritual cataract. As surely as the desire for growth built the complicated alimentary canal from the simplest beginning so that the craving for growth might be satisfied; as surely as the desire for motion evolved the wonderful joints, sinews, and ligaments wherewith this is accomplished; just as surely will the intense yearning to continue the relationships severed by death build the organ for its gratification--the spirit eye. Therefore this wholesale slaughter of millions of men ha helped and is helping more to bridge the gulf between the invisible and the visible world than a thousand years of preaching could do. All through the history of the world it has been recorded that warriors have seen so-called supernatural manifestations, and there is plenty of testimony that those visions have also been seen in the present war. The shock of the wound, the suffering in the hospital, and tears of the widows and orphans, all are opening the spiritual eyes of Europe, and the age of doubt and skepticism will pass away. Instead of being ashamed of having faith in God, the world will honor a man for his piety rather than for his prowess in a not very distant future. And let us all pray for that day.

CYCLIC MOVEMENTS OF THE SUN

THE news printed today in big type on the front pages of newspapers, news which seems of such vital and absorbing interest to everybody, is usually forgotten tomorrow, and the papers that contained the records are thrown into the fire. Likewise the song that is upon the lips of everybody is usually after awhile relegated to he archives of oblivion. Even the men who are launched like meteors into the limelight of publicity are usually soon forgotten, together with the deeds that caused their brief popularity--for, it? quote Solomon, "All is vanity." But among the kaleidoscopic changes that are constantly altering the stage of the world, morally, mentally, and physically, there are certain cyclic events which, though they are recurrent in their nature, have a permanency and stability about them which differentiates the macrocosmic from the microcosmic method of conducting affairs.

In the spring time, at Easter, when the sun crosses the eastern or vernal equinox, the earth emerges from its wintry sleep and shakes off the snowy blanket which has covered it with a vesture of immaculate purity. The voice of nature is heard when the little babbling brooks begin to trickle down the hillside on their way to the great ocean. It is heard when the wind whispers in the newly sprouted forest leaves the song of love that calls forth the bud and the flower which finally bears the pollen that is carried upon invisible wings to the waiting mate. It is heard in the love song of the mating birds and the call of beast unto beast. It continues in every department of nature until the increase of new life has compensated for the destruction by death.

Through the summer, Love and Life toil exceedingly with joyful heart, for they are Masters in the struggle for existence while the sun is exalted in the northern heavens, at the maximum of his power at the summer solstice. Time goes by, and there comes another turning point at the fall equinox. The song of the woodland choir is now hushed; the love call of beast and bird ceases and nature becomes mute again. The light wanes, and the shadows of night grow longer, until at winter solstice, where we are now, the earth again prepares for the deepest sleep, for she need the night of rest after the strenuous activities of the preceding day.

But as the spiritual activities of man are greatest while his body is asleep, so also, by the law of analogy, we may understand that the spiritual fires in the earth are brightest at this time of the year; that now is the best opportunity for soul growth, for investigation and study of the deeper mysteries of life. And therefore it behooves us to catch opportunity on the wing so that we may use this present time to the very best advantage; yet without hurry, without worry, but patiently and prayerfully, knowing that among all other things in the world which change, this great wave of spiritual light will be with us in the winter season for ages to come. It will grow more and more brilliant as the earth and ourselves evolve to higher degrees of spirituality. We are now doing the pioneer work of spreading the Rosicrucian teachings which will help to illuminate the world during the centuries immediately following our present time. There is a law that "you can get only as you give." Now--this season of the year--is the most propitious time to give and receive, so let us be sure to let our light shine on the great cosmic Christmas tree, that it may be seen of men, and that they may be attracted to the truths which we know to be of such vital importance in the development of our fellow men.

In concluding this letter I desire to thank every one of the students for their co-operation in the work during the past year. Any may we do better work together in the coming year.

THE TEACHER'S DEBT OF GRATITUDE

WE are now at the close of another year of our lives and at the beginning of a new, and certain thoughts have come to me in connection with these divisions of our earthly lives.

When Christ was at the end of His ministry, eating the last supper with His disciples, he washed their feet, despite protests from some who thought that this was a humiliation for the teacher. But as a matter of fact it was the symbol of an attitude of mind which is of great significance as a factor in soul growth. Were it not for the mineral soil, the higher plant kingdom would be an impossibility; and the animal kingdom could not exist if the plants did not give it the needed substance. Thus we see that in nature the higher feeds upon and is dependent on the lower for its growth and further evolution. Although it is a fact that the disciples were instructed and helped by Christ, it is also a fact that they were stepping-stones in His development; and it was in recognition of this fact that He humbled Himself, acknowledging His debt to them in the performance of the most menial service imaginable.

It has been the great privilege of the writer to transmit the esoteric instructions of the Elder Brothers to you and thousands of others during the past year, and in this he has been aided by all the workers on Mt. Ecclesia, directly or indirectly. Those who have helped in the print shop, office, or whatever necessary department have all had their share in this privilege, and we all thank you for these opportunities for soul growth which have come to us in satisfying your need.

We trust that we have been of some service in that respect, and ask your prayers that we may become more efficient servants in the coming year.

And how about you, dear friend? During the past year you also have had opportunities to serve others in a similar manner. Have you used your talents of knowledge transmitted to you to enlighten those with whom you have come in contact? It is not necessary to stand in a pulpit, literally or metaphorically, at any time in order to speak to the heart of others. It is often most effectively accomplished in the little quiet ways, such that people do not know we are trying to show them something. We trust you have improved your opportunities to the best of your ability during the past year, and pray that you may enter the new year with a still more earnest spirit of service, and that is may prove to be much more fruitful of soul growth than the past has been.

SPIRITUAL TEACHERS--TRUE AND FALSE

ONE of the most difficult problems which confront the leader of a spiritual movement is the impatience of students who want to reap where they have not sown. They are not patient enough to wait for the harvest but want results immediately, and if they do not sprout wings within a specified time set by themselves they are ready to cry "fraud" and seek and "individual teacher," visible or invisible. So long as he will "guarantee" results, they are prepared to throw common sense to the winds and follow him blindly, though he may lead them to the insane asylum or to a consumptives's grave, or in the cases of those who get off the easiest, simply separate them from some of their cash.

This condition has been dealt with before in letters to students, but there are always some who forget and new students are constantly being added to the class; therefore it is necessary to reiterate important points from time to time. Hearing recently of one who left a certain center for an "individual teacher," and who seems on that account to be envied in a measure by others of the group who have not been so fortunate (?), it seems expedient to go into the matter again.

Have you ever seen any institution, from kindergarten to college, where they keep a teacher for every pupil? We have not. No board of education would sanction such a waste of energy, nor would they appoint an individual teacher for any one simply because that pupil was impatient and wanted to get through school "quick." And finally, even if a board could be found willing to appoint a teacher in a special case who would "cram" knowledge into the pupils brain, there would be a great danger of brain fever, insanity, and maybe death in that method.

If this is true in schools of physical science, how can anyone believe that it can be different with regard to spiritual science? Christ said to His disciples: "If I have told you earthly things, and ye believe not, how shall ye believe, if I tell you of heavenly things?" No "individual teacher," if such there were, can initiate anyone into the mysteries of the soul until the pupil is prepared by his or her own work. Whoever professes to do so brands himself as an impostor of a low order. And whoever allows himself to be so duped shows very little common sense; otherwise he would realize that no truly highly evolved teacher could afford to give his time and energy to the instruction of a single pupil, when he might just as easily teach a large number.

Imagine, if you can, the twelve great Brothers of the Rose Cross, each tagging around after on puny pupil! The thought is a sacrilege. Such truly great and highly evolved men have other and more important things to attend to, and even the lay brothers who have been initiated by them are not allowed to bother them for small and unimportant matters.

It may therefore be stated emphatically that the Elder Brothers do not habitually visit any one in the Rosicrucian Fellowship, or out of it, as an "individual teacher," and whoever thinks so is being deceived. They have given certain teachings which form the basis of instruction in this school, and by learning how to live this silence of the soul we may in time fit ourselves to meet them face to face in the school of Invisible Helpers. There is no other way.

I trust that this may fix the idea more firmly in your own mind than it has been before, and give you a basis for setting others right who are in danger of being side-tracked.

THE BATTLE THAT RAGES WITHIN

FROM time to time we are grieved to receive letters from students in the warring countries chiding us for not taking up the cudgel in favor of their side. There has not been a day since this sad conflict began that we have not mourned the dreadful slaughter, though comforted by the knowledge that it is helping as nothing else could to break down the barrier between the living and the dead. Thus the war will go far towards abolishing the sorrow now experienced by the masses when parting from loved ones; also the present sorrow is turning the Western people from the pleasures of the world to the worship of God. There has not been a night that we have not worked diligently with the dead and wounded to allay their mental anguish or physical pain.

Patriotism was very good at one time, but Christ said, "Before Abraham was, I am." (EGO SUM). Races and nations, comprehended in the term "Abraham," are evanescent, but "the Ego," which existed before Abraham, the race father, will also persist when nations are a thing of the past. Therefore the Fellowship disregards national and racial differences, endeavoring to join all together in a bond of love to fight a Great War--the only war in which a true Christian should fight, and one which a true Christian ought to wage unflinchingly and without quarter--the war against his lower nature. Paul says: "For I know that in me (that is, in my flesh) dwelleth no good thing. For the good that I would, I do not: but the evil which I would not, that I do. I delight in the law of God after the inward man: But I see another law in my members, warring against the law of my mind, and bringing me into captivity to the law of sin which is in my members. O wretched man that I am! Who shall deliver me from the body of this death?" Does not Paul describe here most accurately the state of every aspiring soul? Are we not all suffering spiritually because of the conflict within ourselves? I hope there is but one answer, namely, that this inner war is being waged fiercely and unremittingly by every Fellowship student; for where there is no struggle, there is a sure indication of spiritual coma. The "body of sin" has then the upper hand. But the fiercer the fight, the more hopeful our spiritual state.

In America we hear a great deal of talk of "neutrality" and "preparedness" for "defensive" purposes. In the nobler war which we must wage, there can be no "neutrality." Either there is peace, and "the flesh" rules us and holds us in abject subjections, or there is war aggresively waged by both flesh and spirit. And so long as we continue to live in this "body of death" this warfare will continue, for even Christ was tempted, and we cannot expect to fare better than He.

"Preparedness" is good. It is more necessary every day, for just as a physical enemy seeks to trap and ambush a strong adversary rather than risk open battle, so also the temptations which beset us on "the path" become more subtle with each succeeding year.

Writer like Thomas a Kempis were wont to speak of themselves as "vile worms," and to use kindred terms of "self-abasement," because they knew the great and subtle danger of "self-approbation." But even that may be carried too far, and we may feel that we are "very, very good" and "holier" than others because we abuse ourselves; and we may do it for the pleasure we get from hearing other people contradict us. Truly, the snares of the desire body are past finding out.

There is a way to be prepared, and it is sure: "Look to Christ," and keep your mind busy every waking moment when not engaged in your daily work, studying how you may serve Him. Endeavor by every available means to carry out in a practical manner the ideas thus conceived. The more closely we imitate Christ, the more loyally we follow the dictates of the Higher Self, the more certainly shall we vanquish the lower nature and win the only war worth while winning.

EASTER, A PROMISE OF NEWNESS OF LIFE

THIS is the Easter lesson, though it does not say one word connected with the cosmic event of the present season. But it emphasizes anew the great vital fact that birth and death are only incidents in the life of the spirit, which is without beginning or end.

Old age, sickness, war, or accident may destroy this earthly habitation, but we have "a house from heaven" that no power can move. And so, no matter how closely death may come to us or to our loved ones, we know that as Good Friday is followed by the glorious Easter, so also the door of death is but the gate to a longer life where the sickness and paid which lays our physical body low have no more dominion.

Just think what that means to our poor brothers who are torn and mangled by the awful inhumanity of man to man, and let us give thanks that they have escaped from the suffering which they must have endured if there had been no death to liberate them.

The great majority look upon death as "the king of terrors," but when we are instructed, we realize that under our present conditions death is a friend indeed. None of us has a perfect body, and as it deteriorates in an alarming degree during the few years that we use it, think how it would feel a million years hence--and a million years are less than a fleeting moment compared to infinite duration. None but spirit can endure infinity, and therefore Easter is the earnest of our hope of immortality, and Christ the first fruits of immortality and many brethren with Him.

Let us then, dear friend, approach the coming Easter in an attitude of spiritual aspiration to imitate our great Leader, the Christ, by crucifying our lower nature. May every day of the coming year be a Good Friday, may every night be spent in the purgatorial prison ministering to the spirits there confined, as Christ also did, and may every morn be a glorious Easter on which we rise in the newness of life to greater and better deeds.

"Take care of the pennies and the dollars will look after themselves" says a worldly wise proverb. We may paraphrase and adapt it to the spiritual life by saying, "Take heed that every day is well spent, and the years will yield much treasure."

DAILY EXERCISE IN SOUL CULTURE

WHEN Christ visited Martha and Mary the former was much more concerned with preparation for his material comfort than in attending to the spiritual matters which he taught; hence the rebuke that she was concerned with many things of lesser moment than "the one thing needful." There is no doubt that it is positively wicked to neglect fulfilling one's duties and meeting every obligation honestly incurred in our ordinary everyday life. But unfortunately most of us make the great mistake of looking upon our work and duties in the material world as paramount, thinking that the spiritual side of our development can wait until a convenient time when we have nothing else to do. An increasing number of people admit that they ought to give more attention to spiritual matters, but they always have an excuse for not attending to them just now. "My business requires my entire attention," one will say. "Times are so strenuous, and in order to keep my head above water I must work from early morning till late at night. But as soon as times are a little better I am going to look into these matters and give more time to them." Another claims that certain relatives are dependent on him and that when he has fulfilled his obligations to these dependents he will be able to devote his time to soul growth.

There is no doubt that in many cases these excuses are legitimate, to a certain extent, and that the one who makes them is really and truly sacrificing himself or herself for some one else. I remember the case of a probationer who once wrote in distress that her two little children were always in need of attention at the times when she ought to perform her morning and evening exercises. She ardently desired to progress along the path of the higher life but the care of the children seemed a hindrance, and she asked what she should do. Attend to her children, of course, as I wrote to her. The sacrifice involved in giving up her own progress for the sake of her children's comfort naturally won a rebound to a thousand times more soul growth than if she had neglected her children for her own selfish interests.

But on the other hand there are many who simply lack the mental stamina to make th sustained effort. No matter how strenuous busines conditions are, it is possible to devote a little time each day, morning and evening, to the attainment of spirituality. It is an exceedingly good practice to concentrate the mind upon an ideal during the time spent in street cars going from home to the place of business. The very fact that there is so much noise and confusion, which makes the effort more difficult, is in itself a help; for he who learns to direct his thought one-pointedly under such conditions will have no difficulty in obtaining the same results, or even better, under more favorable circumstances. The time thus spent will prove far more profitable than if used for reading a newspaper or a magazine which will call attention to conditions that are far from elevating.

The mind of most people is like a sieve. As water runs through the sieve so also thoughts flit through their brain. These thoughts are good, bad, and indifferent--mostly the latter. The mind does not hold on to any of them sufficiently long to learn its nature, and yet we are apt to entertain the idea that we cannot help our thoughts being what they are. On that account the great majority have formed the habit of listless thinking which makes them incapable of holding on to any subject until it is thoroughly mastered. It may be difficult to do, but certainly when the power of thought-control has been gained, the possessor holds within his hand the key to success in whatever line he may be engaged.

Therefore I would urge you in connection with this series of lessons, The Occult Effect of the Emotions," which you are receiving that you take the above personally to heart and set aside a portion of each day for the purpose of gaining thought-control. There are a number of helpful hints given by various authors, but i will think the matter over and try to give some general hints. This is very difficult because so much depends upon the temperament of the student. The instruction should really be individual, rather than collective, to bring the best results.

THE REAL HEROES OF THE WORLD

THOUGH my letter is dated the first of the month it was written earlier of course--in fact, the evening before "Decoration Day," the day when all patriotic Americans are supposed to honor the dead heroes who fought for the integrity of the Union.

As I thought over the matter it occurred to me that it seems always to require a calamity or a catastrophe to make me forget self and rise to the call of a cause or to the need of the occasion regardless of consequences. They always respond in war, earthquake, fire, or shipwreck.

But why should it require such cataclysmic events to bring out the virtue of self-sacrificing service when they are needed every day and hour in every home, hamlet, and city? The world would be so much better off if we did our noble deeds daily instead of only on occasion of exceptional stress. It may be noble to die for a great cause, but it is surely nobler to live a life of self-sacrifice, covering many years, cherishing others and helping them to be better and nobler, than to die in the attempt to kill a fellow being.

There is many a father who struggles years and years to give his children what he terms "a chance in life." There are thousands of mothers who toil a lifetime at "hard labor" to aid in this work for the young. There are millions of such heroes who are never heard of because they helped their fellows to live instead of causing them to die.

Is this not an anomaly--that we honor an army of men for more than half a century because they killed, killed, killed, while that greater army which fostered all that is best on earth lie forgotten in their graves? As followers of Christ, let us pay tribute to the heroes and heroines who through years of suffering fought for others by rendering tender care in childhood's helpless days, by unflagging service in times of sickness, by patient participation in poverty and in any and every trouble that might befall.

Nor let us wait till they have passed to the beyond, but let us honor them here and now. Neither should we set one day in the year apart for the payment of such tribute, but we should honor them every day of our lives, and we should seek to lighten their burdens by emulating their noble deeds.

How shall we find them? they wear no uniform, neither do they wear their hearts upon their sleeves. They are everywhere, and if we seek we shall find them. The quicker we join their ranks, the sooner we shall honor ourselves by lightening their burdens as it becomes all true servants of the Master. "Inasmuch as ye have done it unto one of the least of these my brethren, ye have done it unto me."

THE WORK OF THE RACE SPIRITS

IN a few days we shall celebrate in America "The Glorious Fourth," our Independence Day, and we shall waste a lot of perfectly good and useful powder that might be put to better use, in order to show our "patriotism." A considerable number of fires and accidents will occur if we may judge from many precedents.

To what purpose all of this we may see by the heartrending spectacle of the war which for almost two years has made tears a mockery, for no symbol of sorrow is adequate to the occasion. let us realize that had there been no "patriotism," there could have been no war; and realizing its baneful influence, let us learn to say with Thomas Paine, "The world is my country, and to do good is my religion." This, it seems to me, is the gospel we ought to preach to our fellow men in whatever country we happen to be, for this attitude of mind will be one of the factors in accomplishing our emancipation from the Race Spirit feeds on war, for it causes the nation which it rules to sink its internal differences for the time being and its people to cluster close to one another for defense or aggression against the common foe. Thus they vibrate in harmony to an extent greater than usual, and this strengthens the Race Spirit and delays the advent of Christ to that extent. So long as patriotism holds the nations in bondage to the Race Spirits, the Universal Kingdom cannot be started.

I would therefore urge that the students of the Rosicrucian Fellowship refrain from participation in any patriotic exercises of a martial nature. Practice Universal Brotherhood by never mentioning or recognizing differences of nationality, for we are all one in Christ.

STRUGGLES OF THE ASPIRING SOUL

FROM time to time letters of discouragement are received at Headquarters from people who are smitten by conscience because they are unable to live up to their high ideals, and they feel that it would be more honest to abandon the faith and live as others live who make no professions. They say that while they read and study or listen in church to passages which exhort them to love their enemies, to bless them that curse them, and to pray for those who despitefully use them, they are heart and soul in accord with these sentiments and would gladly follow these precepts; but when they meet such conditions in the world, they cannot comply with the Biblical command, and therefore feel that they are hypocrites.

If man were a homogeneous whole, if spirit, soul, and body were one and undivided, that these people are hypocrites would be true. But spirit, soul, and body are not one, as we realize to our sorrow from the very first day that we feel the desire to tread the path of the higher life. And in this fact lies the solution of the problem. There are two distance natures in each of us. In the days of our unaspiring life the higher spiritual nature is asleep, and the worldly personal self is undisputed lord of all our actions. Then there is peace and serenity. But the moment the spiritual nature wakens, the war begins. As we grow in spirituality, the struggle is intensified until some time in the future the personality will succumb, and we shall gain the peace that passeth all understanding.

In the meantime we have the condition whereof our students complain (with Paul, Faust, and every other aspiring soul), that to will is easy, but that the good that they would, they do not, and the evil that they would not, that they do. The writer has felt, and feels most keenly every day of his life this discrepancy between this teachings and his actions. One part of his being aspires with an ardor that is painful in its intensity to all the higher and nobler things, while on the other hand, a strong personality, exceedingly difficult to curb, is a source of continual grief. But he feels that so long as he does not "pose" as a saint, so long as he honestly admits his shortcomings and professes his sorrow for them, and so long as he uses the inclusive "WE" in all his exhortations, he deceives no one, and is not a hypocrite. Whatever he says he takes to himself first and foremost, and, however, unsuccessful, he strive to follow the Rosicrucian teachings. If everyone else among our students feels troubled on the same score as the correspondents who have inspired this letter, we hope that this may set them right.

Besides, what else can we do but go on? Having once awakened the higher nature, it cannot be permanently silenced, and there will be the misery of regret and remorse if we abandon effort. We have several times called attention to the way the mariner guides his vessel across the waste of waters by a star. He will never reach it, but nevertheless it brings him safely through the rock shoals to the desired haven. Similarly, if our ideals are so high that we realize we shall never reach them in this life, let us also keep in mind that we have endless time before us, and that what we cannot accomplish in this life-day will be achieved tomorrow or later. Let us follow the example of Paul and "by patient persistence in well-doing" continue to seek for spiritual glory, honor, and immortality.

BUILDING FOR THE FUTURE LIFE

YOU know of course that the Fellowship teaches rebirth to be a fact in nature, and you believe in this doctrine because it explains so many facts in life which we are otherwise unable to account for. But I wonder how many students have really taken the practical use of this truth to heart, and are fixing their attention upon it by consciously and systematically molding themselves and thus making their environment for future lives.

It is true that in the Second Heaven we devote all of our time to making the environment for our future life, forming the earth and the sea, providing the conditions for the flora and fauna, and generally shaping things to give us a suitable arena for our coming life work. But we do that according to the way we have been living here in this present life. If we have been lazy and shiftless here, living in a happy-go-lucky manner, it is not likely that when we come to the Second Heaven we will be careful to prepare a fertile soil, which we may later till. Therefore our next embodiment will probably find us with the barest means of existence at hand, so that under the whip of necessity we may learn to exert ourselves.

It is similar with our moral qualities. When we are ready to descend into the next embodiment, we can only build into our new vehicles what we have garnered in this. Therefore it is wise for us to commence now, when our next life is in the moldable clay stage, to make our ideals what we would like them to be and to make the environment in which we would like to be raised.

We are without a doubt all ready to agree in the first place than our present bodies are not as we wish them. Diseases of all sorts come to most people; some are subject to pain all their lives, and no one is ever able to go through life from the cradle to the grave without having at least some suffering. Thus each one of us may well picture himself in a future life with a healthy body in which he will be free from diseases that are now his worst plague.

With respect to the moral and mental faculties we are also far from perfect, and each one may therefore take up with profit the subject of improvement in that direction. Do we realize that we have a critical spirit, a sharp tongue, a hasty temper, or other kindred faults which bring us into trouble with others and make life unpleasant in our environment? Very well; by holding in mind and visualizing our ideal self for the future--having equipose under all circumstances, being soft-spoken, kindly, and affectionate, etc.--we shall build these ideals into the thought form we have already shaped for ourselves in that distant day. And according to the intensity of the concentration which we apply tot he matter will be the result. In so far as we endeavor now to cultivate and aspire virtues, we shall possess them then; and this applies to faculties as well. If we are solely now, by the aspiration to maintain order we shall later bring back that virtue. Are we lacking the sense of ryhthm? Very well, it may be ours in the future by asking now. Mechanical ability, or any thing else that is necessary to give us the life experience we seek, may be had in the same way.

Therefore we ought systematically to set aside a certain time at intervals, as frequent as is consistent with our other duties, to think forward and plan for future life--what sort of a body, what faculties, virtues, and environment we wish. When we are able to make our choice intelligently, we are undoubtedly given a great deal more latitude than if we had not thought about the matter at all.

You understand of course that the highest form of aspiration to virtue is the constant endeavor to practice in it our daily lives. But while we are endeavoring to cultivate virtues, as we should, by practice, it is scientific to plan ahead the use we shall make of the future life just as we now plan ahead the use of the day that is before us. I trust that this idea may take root among the students and be consistently carried to its legitimate consummation, for in that way it will be bound to have a wonderful effect upon the future of ourselves and the future of the world about us.

DESCENT OF THE CHRIST LIFE IN THE FALL

WE are now at the fall equinox where the physical sun is leaving the northern hemisphere after having provided us with the necessities of life for the coming year; and the spiritual tide which carries on its crest the life which will find physical expression in the coming year is now on its way towards our earth. The half-year directly before us is the holy part of the year. From the feast of the Immaculate Conception to the Mystic Birth at Christmas (while this wave is descending into the earth) and from that time to Easter (while it is traveling outward) a harmonious, rhythmic vibratory song, not inaptly described in the legend of the Mystic Birth as a "hosanna" sung by an angel choir, fills the planetary atmosphere and acts upon all as an impulse to spiritual aspiration. Not upon all in even measure, of course, but according to their general character.

Some do not feel this spiritual save at all because of their depravity, but it works in, on, and with them just the same, and in time they will respond. Others are so engrossed in their buying and selling, their marrying and giving in marriage, their loves and their ambitions, that they are not conscious of it save at the time when it is at its maximum strength, namely, namely, Christmas, and then it expresses itself only as a spirit of super-sociability and generosity; they like to feast and give presents. A more advanced class feels the wave of holiness from the very beginning of its descent, and realizes the important effect of its harmony and rhythm in furthering efforts in the direction of soul growth. They profit accordingly by making the most efforts during the months from the fall to the spring equinox. It is like swimming with the tide.

For that reason I am devoting this letter to call your attention tot he annually recurring phenomenon. Whether you are conscious of it or not, the powerful spiritual vibrations of life-giving Christ wave are in the earth's atmosphere during the winter months, and may be used by you to a much greater advantage if you know it and double your efforts than if you are unaware of the fact.

Let us therefore each take stock of the particular sins which most easily beset us, for now is beginning the most favorable time of the year for their eradication. Let us also take stock of the virtues we lack and feel most need of cultivating, for this is the time to do the work most efficiently. By careful, systematic work in the holy winter months we may make great strides in our efforts to realize our spiritual aspirations.

Having made up our minds as to the personal work, let us look about us to see who in our circle of acquaintances seem to be seeking for spiritual enlightenment, and who would be likely to lend an ear to our teachings. This requires discrimination, for we have no right to force our ideas upon unwilling ears any more than we would be justified in beating a drum in their rooms for an hour or two each day. If we find that they do not take kindly to what we have to say, it is better to leave them; but there are many who may be awakened in winter under the spiritual Christ vibration who could not be reached in summer. I therefore trust that we may use all the coming months in a way which shall profit us greatly from the spiritual standpoint.

THE REASON FOR THE TRIALS THAT BESET THE OCCULT STUDENT

FROM time to time we receive letters from students complaining that since they have taken up the higher teachings, and are trying to live in conformity with them, everything seems to go wrong with their affairs. Some feel a determined opposition in their homes, others suffer in business, and some are even affected in health. Some, according to temperament, are ready to give up, and others grit their teeth in persistence in well-doing" despite the trials. But all are unanimous in asking why this marked change in their affairs. Each receives the best help we can given to solve his individual problems, but as we feel that there are many among the students who have been similarly tried, it seems appropriate to state the reason for this condition.

In the first place, the aspiring soul should realize that the adverse conditions happen for good according to a firmly established law of nature whereby God aims to aid him in the quest. Trials are a sign of progress and a cause for great rejoicing. This is how the law acts: During all our past lives we have made ties and have incurred debts under the Law of Causation. These debts continue to increase so long as we live the usual selfish, haphazard lives, and we may liken each debt to a drop of vinegar. When the turning point comes and we cease to make vinegar, the law of justice requires that we take our medicine. But we are allowed to determine whether we will take it in large doses and have it over quickly or whether we prefer to take it in very small sips and string it out over a number of lives. This choice is not made by words but by acts. If we take up the work of self-improvement with enthusiasm, if we cut our vices out by the roots and LIVE the life we profess, the Great Beings whom we know as the Recording Angels give us a stronger dose of vinegar than they would if we merely talked about the beauties of the higher life. They do that to help us toward the day of liberation from our self-made bonds and not to harm or hinder us.

In view of these facts we can understand the Christ's exhortation to rejoice when men revile us and accuse us falsely for His sake. Boys pass a barren tree with indifference, but as soon as the tree bears fruit, they are ready to throw stones and rob it. So it is with men also: while we walk with the crowd and do as they do, we are unmolested, but the moment we do what they know in their hearts to be right, we become a living reproach to them even if we never utter a word of censure, and in order to justify themselves in their own eyes they begin to find fault with us. In this respect those who are most closely associated with us in the home or in business are more prominent than strangers who have no connection with us. But whatever the form or the source of such trouble it is a cause for congratulation, for it shows that we are doing something effectively progressive; so let us keep on undismayed and with unflagging zeal.

SPIRITUAL STOCK-TAKING DURING THE HOLY SEASON

CHRIST likened the aspiring souls of His time to stewards who had received a certain number of talents from their lord and were supposed to go into trade with them that they might increase the capital entrusted to their care. We understand from this parable that all who aspire to serve Him are required likewise to use their God-given talents in such a manner that they show a gain in soul growth when in due season they are called upon to give an account of their stewardship.

This accounting, so far as the majority of mankind is concerned, is put off till the Reaper has closed the ledger of life and they find themselves in Purgatory to receive the result of the things done in the body, whether they be good or ill.

But what would we think of a business man who pursued such a reckless method of conducting his affairs? Would we not feel that he was steering straight for the rock of bankruptcy if he did not balance accounts and take stock of his assets and liabilities every year? Surely we would feel that he deserved to fail because of his neglect to follow ordinary business methods.

If we realize the value of system and the benefit of constantly knowing clearly how we stand with respect to our material affairs, we ought also to pursue the same safe methods regarding our spiritual affairs. Nay, we should be much more circumspect in the conduct of the heavenly matters than in worldly matters, for our material prosperity is but a watch in the night compared to the eternal welfare of the spirit.

We are nearing the winter solstice, which is the beginning of a new year from the spiritual point of view, and we are looking forward to the new outpouring of love from our Father in Heaven through the Christ Child. This, therefore, is a good time to take stock and ask ourselves how we have spent the love offerings of last year, how we have exerted ourselves to gather treasure in heaven. And we shall experience great profit if we approach this stock-taking in the proper spirit and at the most auspicious time, for there is a time to sow and a time to reap, and for everything under the sun there is a time when it may be done with greater chance of success than at any other season.

The stars are the heavenly time markers. From them come the forces which influence us through life. On Holy Night, between the 24th and 25th of December, at midnight, in the place where you live, you will find that retrospection and the resolutions engendered by it for the new year will be most effective.

At Mt. Ecclesia and the various Study Centers a Midnight Service is held on Holy Night, and students attending such services are thereby debarred from the midnight self-communion. Others may be unable to hold it at that time for other reasons. For these any of the late evening or early morning hours will serve nearly as well. But let us all unite on that night in a concerted spiritual effort of aspiration; and let each student not only pray for his individual soul growth in the coming year, but let all unite in a prayer for the collective growth of our movement. The workers at Headquarters also request your helpful thoughts.

If we all put our shoulders to the wheel at this time, we may be sure of an unusually individual and collective blessing and a spiritually prosperous year.

ALL OCCULT DEVELOPMENT BEGINS WITH THE VITAL BODY

RECENTLY a friend who has been taking the correspondence course a number of months wrote to get a matter cleared up which is bothering him; and as it may be that others are feeling somewhat similar to him but have not reached the point of expression, we thought best to use this letter as an answer. It has sufficient general interest to be of value even to those who have not looked at the matter in the light seen by our friend. He does not want to complain, but he asked for the correspondence course in the hope of getting something to further occult development. Instead he receives each month a nice little sermon, which he admits is good for both beginners and advanced students, but where is the schooling? Other authors give certain exercises which help their followers; will we please give him one that will develop the faculty of writing? No, we cannot do that. The Rosicrucian teachings are designed to further spiritual progress rather than material prosperity, and we know of no occult exercise which will bring wealth, either directly or by abnormally fostering a latent talent. If we did, we would not teach it, for such use of occult power is black magic. "Seek ye first the kingdom of God and His righteousness, and all these things shall be added unto you," said Christ, and we shall make no mistake by following His advice. If our friend or any one else wants to develop a latent faculty for the good alone he may do with it, that spiritual aspiration will, if persistently adhered to and backed by physical effort (works), eventually bring the desired end without the need of a special occult exercise.

And about the lessons being "nice little sermons." Yes, so they are when read superficially. But if they are studied deeply, there is a great deal of occult knowledge found of much more benefit to the student than an exercise such as the one our friend wants. There is, however, "method in our madness" in giving it out just that way. Perhaps this may not have been apparent to students, and we will therefore try to make it clear. Kindly bear in mind, however, that the following is a comparison made for a legitimate purpose; it is not a criticism.

Apart from the fact that the Eastern School of Occultism bases its teachings on Hinduism, while the Western Wisdom School espouses Christianity, the religion of the West, there is ONE GREAT FUNDAMENTAL, IRRECONCILABLE DISCREPANCY between the teachings of the modern representatives of the East and those of Rosicrucians. According to the version of Eastern Occultism the vital body--which is called "LINYA SHARIRA"--is comparatively unimportant, for it is incapable of development as a vehicle of consciousness. It serves only as an avenue for the solar force "prana," and as "a link" between the physical body and the desire body, which is called "KAMA RUPA," also the "astral body." this, they say, is the vehicle of the Invisible Helper.

The Western Wisdom School teaches us as its fundamental maxim that "ALL OCCULT DEVELOPMENT BEGINS WITH THE VITAL BODY," and the writer, as its public representative, has therefore been busy since the inception of our movement trying to gather and disseminate knowledge concerning the four ethers and the vital body. Much information was given in the "COSMO" and succeeding book, but the monthly lessons and letters give the result of our researches up to date. We are constantly parading this vital body (vital in a double sense) before the minds of the students so that by knowing and thinking about it as well as by reading and heeding the "nice little sermons" which we use to wrap this information in, they may consciously, and unconsciously, weave the "Golden Wedding Garment." We would advise all to study these lessons carefully year after year; there may be much dross, but there is gold among them.

You have our sincere wishes for abundant spiritual growth during the New Year.

SERVING WHERE BEST FITTED TO SERVE

A question was asked recently as follows: "You speak so much about SERVICE; just what does that mean? There are in our Fellowship a number of people who say that they love to serve, but they do not do anything but what they like to do. Is that service?" It seems that this question offers food for profitable thought and that an analysis of the subject may benefit us all, so we decided to devote the monthly letter to this purpose.

It is evident that they majority of people in the world will not serve unless there is "something in it" for them. They are looking for a material reward, and that is the wise way of the unseen powers to spur them to action, for thus they are unconsciously evolving toward the stage in soul growth where they will serve for the love of serving. But they cannot be expected to change over night; there are no sudden transformations in nature. When the eggshell bursts and a chicken walks out, of when the cocoon breaks and a butterfly wings it was among the flowers, we know that the magic was not wrought in a moment. There was an inner process of preparation prior to the outward change. A similar process of inner growth is required to change the servants of Mammon to servants of Love.

If we want to make a building larger, all we have to do is to bring our brick and other building material to the place, start a force of workmen, and presto! the building begins to grow apace to any dimensions we desire and at any speed we wish, depending only upon our ability to furnish labor and material. But if we want to increase the size of a tree or an animal, we cannot accomplish our object by nailing wood to the tree trunk or lading flesh and skin upon the back of the animal. The building grows by external accretions, but in all living things physical growth is from within and cannot be hurried to any appreciable extent without danger of complication. It is the same with spiritual growth; it proceeds from within and must have time. We cannot expect that people who have just begun to feel the inner urge impelling them into an altruistic association, to renounce in the twinkling of an eye all selfishness and other vices and blossom out into the stature of Christ. At best we are only just a little better than we were save for the fact that we are striving and endeavoring to follow "in His steps." But that makes all the difference, for we are TRYING to serve as He served.

If that is the motive, it in nowise detracts from the service of a musician who inspires us with devotion at our services that he loves his music. Nor does it render the service any less because the speaker who fires us with zeal in the Master's work loves to clothe his ideas in beautiful words. Nor does it make the hall less attractive because the member who swept, dusted, and decorated it loves to make his exterior surroundings beautiful. Each can, in fact, serve to much better advantage if the line of service lies along the path of his natural inclinations and abilities, and we ought to encourage one another to look for opportunities in the line where each is best fitted to serve.

There is no special merit in seeking out service in a capacity that is disagreeable to us. It would be a mistake if the musician said to the caretaker: "I dislike to scrub floors and decorate rooms, and I know you tremble at the thought of playing, also that you are out of practice, but let us change places for the sake of service." On the other hand, if no one were there to play, it would be the decorator's duty to put diffidence aside and serve as well as possible. If the floor needed scrubbing and the chairs dusting, the speaker and musician should be willing to do that work also regardless of personal dislike. Nothing is menial. The same principle will apply in the home, shop, or office. SERVICE MAY BE DEFINED AS THE BEST USE OF OUR TALENTS--THE PUTTING OF OUR TALENTS TO THE BEST USE IN EACH CASE OF IMMEDIATE NEED REGARDLESS OF LIKE OR DISLIKE.

If we strive to do this, our progress and soul growth will increase correspondingly.

"LOST SOULS" AND STRAGGLERS

WE have been asked to give a lesson on "lost souls" and stragglers. Our correspondent wants to know the Rosicrucian teachings concerning them. As this very question was dealt with earlier in this book, in the letter for April, 1912 (No. 17), we cannot do better than refer our correspondent to it. We trust that it will explain the matter to him. We should be glad if other students who have questions of general interest would submit them for elucidation in these letters, for although there is a question of department in the "Rays," not all our students are subscribers. Also the problems presented can perhaps be given a little more intimate treatment here than is possible in a magazine that must go before a public which is not as well versed in the philosophy as our students.

THE UNNECESSARY FEAR OF DEATH

IT is really pathetic to see the gloom of people who have been bereaved by the death of some one near and dear, and to see how in extreme cases they devote themselves for the rest of their lives to mourning for the one who has passed on. They clothe themselves in sable garments, and deem it a sacrilege to the memory of the departed one to even smile, little realizing that by such an attitude of mind they are keeping in the densest regions of the invisible world the person whom they profess to love, where all that is evil lives and moves and has its being in close contact with the base and selfish side of humanity. This is not a mere fancy but an actual fact, demonstrable to any one who has the slightest extension of the physical sight.

It is one of the greatest blessings conferred upon those who study and believe the Rosicrucian teachings that they are gradually emancipated from the fear of death and from the feeling that a great calamity has happened when some one near and dear to them passes into the invisible beyond. A blessing flows both to the so-called "living" and the so-called "dead" when the departing spirit is given the proper care and help during the transition. It is then able to assimilate the panorama of live, which will make the post-mortem existence full and profitable because undisturbed by the sorrow, grief, and hysterical weeping of those who are still in the body. During the years which follow it may also be assisted by their prayers.

On the other hand, those of the so-called "living" who study these teachings are learning to practice this unselfish attitude toward death, so necessary to soul growth, because they realize that as a matter of actual fact death of the body at the proper time is the greatest blessing that can befall humanity. There is not one among us who has a body so perfect that it is fit to be lived in forever. In most cases the passing years bring out the weak points in our vehicles to an increasing degree, crystallizing and hardening them so that they become more and more of a burden which we are only too glad to lay down. Then we have the hope and the knowledge that we shall be given a new body and a new start in a future age, so that we may learn more of the lessons in life's school.

This is the time of the year when the Mystic Death which we are all celebrating naturally turns our thoughts and the thoughts of humanity in general to the subject of death and rebirth. There is no other teaching than that of rebirth which is of equally vital importance or of similar value. Humanity needs it at this time more than ever on account of the carnival of cruelty and slaughter that has been enacted in the past two and a half years in Europe. So closely is the human family interconnected that there are probably comparatively few persons in the world who have not lost some relatives in that titanic struggle.

It is at once the duty and the privilege of those who know the truth about death to disseminate it as much as possible among those who are still in darkness concerning the facts connected with this event. Therefore I would urge upon the students of the Rosicrucian Fellowship to realize that we are all stewards of everything we have, mental as well as physical property, and that it is our duty in so far as it is possible in a tactful and diplomatic manner to bring these great facts of life and being to the knowledge of those who are still without them. We never can tell when we cast our bread upon the waters how it will return to us. It is certain that sooner or later these teachings, temporarily forgotten, must again become the knowledge of all humanity, and we ought to share the pearl of knowledge which we have found with others whenever it is possible to do so. If we neglect to do this, we are really committing a sin of omission for which we must sometime answer.

I trust that you will take this to heart and devote yourself to spreading this knowledge, not as time and opportunity offer, but taking time by the forelock and making the opportunity; but with all proper tactfulness so that the object we have in view may not be frustrated by using the wrong method. Furthermore, it is not necessary to label this knowledge. Bible instances can be brought forth to show that this doctrine was believed by the Elders of Israel who sent messengers to John the Baptist to ask if he were Elias. Also their speculations as to whether Christ was Moses, Jeremiah, or another of the prophets are evidence of their belief. Christ believed in rebirth, because He stated definitely that John the Baptist was Elias. This doctrine was enunciated by Paul in the 15th chapter of 1st Corinthians, also in other places.

You can render no greater service to humanity than by teaching them these truths.

HEART DEVELOPMENT AND INITIATION

WHILE I was dictating this month's lesson it occurred to me to ask whether you are getting the full benefit from the lessons or not? It all depends upon the way you are studying, for you cannot get any more out of them than what you put into them yourself. Therefore I thought best to devote this letter to a little discussion of the proper method of using them with maximum benefit.

You know that it is the aim of the Rosicrucian teachings to develop the mind and the heart equally; to give all explanations in such a logical manner than the mind is ready to accept, and then the heart is allowed free scope for working over the material thus received. If you simply read the lesson and think over it and find it reasonable as an explanation of the subject taken up each month, and then you lay it away and forget all about it, it will do you very little good, for you have used only your intellect and not your heart. The proper way, after the lesson has been intellectually assimilated and assented to, is to take it up in a devotional manner during the rest of the month at different times when you feel in the mood for such an exercise. You should then go over the lesson, endeavoring not to think about it at all, leaving the intellect out as far as possible. Endeavor to FEEL it, for feeling is a function of the heart. Try to visualize the different things and subjects taken up in it.

For instance, the lesson which accompanies this present letter deals with humanity during the heraphrodite stage. It calls to mind the entrance of the Lucifer spirits, also the path of regeneration under the guidance of Mercury. If you will visualize before your inner eyes the condition of man during the different stages which have passed, you will reap great benefit. You can do that better than you can visualize and feel the changes that are still in the future, for within your consciousness there lie latent all the feelings that you have had during all the past ages of your evolution, and it is only a matter of practice to be able to call them up at will.

You will remember from what it said in the ROSICRUCIAN COSMO-CONCEPTION concerning the method of Initiation that sometime when you come to that point you will have to travel backward over the road that you have come, and feel and see consciously that which you were unconscious of when you went over it. So the above practice is preparation. The more you can see yourself in the state of mind indicated, the more deeply you can FEEL yourself in the corresponding condition and realize the protecting and guiding hand of the divine hierarchies which have aided us in the path of evolution, the better you will be prepared for the time to come when you are to go through this during the process of Initiation. It is safe to say that you will receive much more benefit from Initiation then than if you are unprepared. this practice of feeling the lesson you will find a very, very great aid to spiritual progress; and properly used, it will illuminate the lessons and give you a spiritual insight that cannot be attained in any other way. Therefore, I sincerely hope that you will take this to heart and make up your mind to practice it regularly, even with lessons which may seem to you at first glance dull and uninteresting. This process will enable you to dig out pearls hidden beneath the surface, of which you have never dreamed.

SACRIFICE AND SPIRITUAL PROGRESS

FROM time to time letters are received at Headquarters asking in various terms the question: "How can I make more spiritual progress?" I have therefore thought well to devote this letter to a consideration of this subject.

It is a law in nature that "from nothing, nothing comes" Yet a great many people labor under the fallacy that spiritual truth and advancement may be had without money and without price. In a certain sense that is true, because it is absolutely wrong and vile to barter spiritual power for fitlhly lucre, as was so forcefully shown by Peter when he dealt with Simon the sorcerer, who wanted to buy spiritual powers from him and offered him money in exchange. At the same time there is a definite price upon spiritual growth which must be paid by every one who wants to attain it. In the first place, the old interests must be sacrificed. We all remember the parable about those who were bidden to the feast of the king but who refrained from coming for various reasons. One had taken a wife and wanted to enjoy his honeymoon; another had bought oxen and wanted to inspect his new property; and so on, with the result that they all neglected their opportunity and lost their chance of advancement.

The same proposition comes to us today in different guise. We may be willing to sit at home and read a book about spiritual things in our leisure hours when we have nothing to do that interest us more, but when the Great Work demands some of our time, we have various excuses. "I have a daughter I want to send through college," says one. "When that is done and my obligations are liquidated, I will take hold." Another says: "My business needs my presence every day, and at night I am tired. I cannot work for the Fellowship in the evening or attend their meetings, for I would not be fit to give all my energies to my work next day. But when I retire from business, I will take hold. A third says: "I have many children who demand my attention and attendance at various social functions. I cannot go to the Fellowship meetings and neglect them. But when they are married, I will work for the cause." It is perfectly true that when we have assumed obligations we must discharge them to the best of our ability. At the same time there is also more than a possibility that if we think thoroughly over the matter we will find that we have some time left from our duties which may be devoted to the Great Work. In this connection it may be well to remember the incident of some coming to Christ and saying to Him: "Thy mother and they brethren stand without, desiring to speak with Thee." He answered, "Who is my mother? and who are my brethren?....Whosoever shall do the will of my Father which is in Heaven, the same is my brother, and sister, and mother." Again He said: "If any man come to Me, and hate not his Father, mother, and wife, and children, and brethren, and sisters, yea and his own life also, he cannot be my disciple. And every one that hath foresaken houses, or brethren, or sisters, or Father, or mother, or wife, or children, or lands, for My Name's sake, shall receive an hundredfold, and shall inherit everlasting life." There is and must be a sacrifice involved in the regenerate life. It has been my experience personally, and in watching thousands of others, that in the direct proportion that any one gives of his thoughts, his time and money to the cause he has espoused so will he reap spiritual benefit. When one consecrates all that he is to the regenerate life and follows the guidance of the spirit it will soon be seen that his very intensity of purpose in the new direction shuts out the old things. He has no longer time for them.

They pass out of his thoughts and drop away. In one way or another the daughter gets through college or finds some equally suitable employment. The business prospers even better than when the proprietor devoted all his time and all his energies to worrying and money grubbing. The children find another chaperon fully as capable as their mother when sometimes she is working for the spiritual cause. In every case that which we give up for the work's sake, the time that we spend in the cause of Christ, and the money we expend in discriminate charity are all provided for and compensated for under the law that works for good.

As the psalmist says: "I have been young, and now am old; yet have I not seen the righteous foresaken, nor his seed begging bread." The law enunciated by Christ, "Seek ye first the Kingdom of God, and His righteousness, and all these things shall be added unto you," holds good in this day as well as when it was spoken. This I have found by actual experience, and every one else who lives the life and does the work will find that the same holds good in his or her case. There is growth only in service.

ADJUSTING THE TEACHINGS TO THE UNDERSTANDING OF OTHERS

RECENTLY we received a letter from Seattle which gives good a suggestion that you may like to use. Our friend writes: "The other day while in Ballard I went into the library and called for the "COSMO." When I was ready to go, I turned over to the table of food values and took the open book up to the librarian's desk. I showed her this table and said: 'This is a valuable table.' She, examining it said: 'Why, I have been asked a number of times for tables of just this kind.' Then the thought came to me that when other students go into a library and ask for the "COSMO,: they might do the same as I had done. The librarian might then catalogue the book as containing hints on health and food, and in that way it might come into the hands of some who are seeking for just the light which it contains." This is true to a much greater extent than we usually realize. Wonderful are the ways and the means and the places in which the Light strikes us, not only when we are not seeking consciously for it but even asserting that there is no such thing as light in the spiritual sense and decrying as frauds those who follow it. It has often been an inspiration and a source of great encouragement to me to think of Paul's journey to Damascus. He was a man who glorified in the zeal wherewith he perse-cuted the saints. None was as diligent as he in putting down that which he believed to be a damnable heresy. But strong souls are the darlings of the gods whether they work for good or for evil, because that indomitable, irresistible energy which drives them to action, even if temporarily used for bad purposes, will be just as strong when diverted into the channels of good. And so Paul was a special favorite of the gods, and therefore was given such a powerful light that it blinded him when he was least looking for such a thing, namely, while on the road to Damascus. Then and there he was given an understanding and a knowledge far superior to those of any of the other apostles. He was chosen for a special mission and given a particular gift in the shape of spiritual vision and the ability to be all things to all men.

Not infrequently our students complain that they cannot make their associates or relatives understand the teachings of the Rosicrucians. An illustration occurred to me the other day when I was looking through the tool chest on Mt. Ecclesia. There were a large number of wrenches in it, some large and some small, each one fitted to turn just one size bolt; there were also a few that were adjustable within certain limits. Now it occurred to me that sometimes a very small wrench may be far more valuable than one of large dimensions; it all depends upon the size of the bolt. For a small bolt you need the small wrench, and for a large one the large wrench. Similarly, when we meet people in the world, we must size them up and see what they require. Many of us have studied very deeply into the Mystery Teachings and have acquired a profound knowledge of these subjects. We are like large wrenches, but absolutely useless for turning the little bolts that have not been touched with this knowledge at all. In such cases we must not try to air our profound knowledge and talk over the heads of our audiences, but we must endeavor to come down to their level and explain things to them in exactly the same elementary manner that was required with us in the beginning.

In other words, we must be adjustable, like some of those wrenches in our tool chest. When we meet an audience of strangers, we must talk right down to their level and use the simplest language possible. Then, again, when we meet older students and are in a class where they are capable of grasping the profounder problems, we may expand to the very fullest of our ability with considerable profit and benefit to ourselves and all others concerned. But above all we must learn, with Paul, to be all things to all men, or we shall defeat the object we have in view of bringing light to seeking souls.

THE VALUE OF REVIEWING PAST LESSONS

THERE is in the following letter a valuable suggestion from a student of the Rosicrucian teachings, which I feel it a duty to pass on: "Last night when looking over a big budget of correspondence that it had been my good fortune to receive from the Fellowship during nearly five years, I wondered how other probationers and students deal with their monthly Fellowship letters. Next it occurred to me that this should be made point of in one of the monthly letters. It is not my desire to criticize the doings of other probationers, but it is very probable that few students and probationers ever realize fully what a mine of information is really contained in these letters, which can be turned into heavenly treasure by right action. How often on looking over back numbers of them have new ideas and realizations sprung into being that I was not conscious of before, and what a help they have been in many an inner struggle! "Truly it may be said that in these back lessons we have a gold mine from which many treasures could be dug that would help us to live the life. Here indeed we have a second COSMO. Truly it behooves students and probationers to correctly file and look after every detail of their correspondence with the Fellowship so that it can be made of as much use as possible in diffusing the light of the Elder Brothers. Perhaps just one of these lessons is all that is required to help a friend. Much benefit must come from an orderly arrangement of them.

"I think it scarcely possible that the majority of students and probationers can ever fully realize what a power for good there is behind these lessons. To those among us who have been used to strict data and scientific methods of research these back lessons will go a long way towards helping unite head and heart. They contain many a gem of thought which will make for right action and perseverance in well-doing. If the students and probationers will hold the thought of how best to use the letters they receive, it will be very helpful and make for more soul growth. Surely it is the little things that make the big things possible, and perhaps this would stir some members to service." If students will bear in mind that repetition is the keynote of the vital body, and that "all occult development begins with the vital body," they will realize why it is so profitable to go over the back lessons and letters frequently.

TAMING AN UNRULY MEMBER

AS you probably know, we have here on Mt. Ecclesia a short service morning and evening, which includes a reading from the Bible. Mrs. Heindel and myself are very fond of reading from time to time the third chapter of James because we find there such an important lesson. I thought it might be well to call it to your attention, particularly because of an incident which happened here a short time ago that served to drive that lesson with great force into my consciousness. I believe that we shall all be able to profit by taking that lesson to heart. Let me quote a few verses from the chapter mentioned, and then I shall tell you the incident to which I refer.

"If any man offend not in word, the same is a perfect man, and able also to bridle the whole body. Behold, we put bits in the horses' mouths that they may obey us; and we turn about their whole body. Behold also the ships, which though they be so great, and are driven of fierce winds, yet are they turned about with a very small helm, whithersoever the governor listeth. Even so the tongue is a little member, and boasteth great things. Behold, how great a matter a little fire kindeth! And the tongue is a fire, a world of iniquity; so is the tongue among our members, that it defileth the whole body, and setteth on fire the course of nature; and it is set on fire of hell, For every kind of beast, and of birds, and of serpents, and of things in the sea is tamed, and hath been tamed of mankind: but the tongue can no man tame; it is an unruly evil, full of deadly poison. Therewith bless we God, even the Father; and therewith curse we men, which are made after the similtude of God. My brethren, these things ought not to be. For where envying and strife is, there is confusion and every evil work. But the wisdom that is from above is first pure, then peaceable, gentle, and easy to be entreated, full of mercy and good fruits. And the fruit of righteousness is sown in peace of them that make peace." We have on Mt. Ecclesia several swarms of bees. Some time ago the gardeners were endeavoring to move a swarm from one place to another. The bees became enraged at this interference with their life and work; they stung their aggressors severely and painfully in a number of places. When this incident was reported to me and I thought it over, it struck me that there was in it a very important lesson. The bee loses its sting whenever it has stung, and then it dies. Just think of it! How strictly the law of justice deals with it! It automatically kills itself when harming anyone else. It is not an avenging God but its own act that brings the retribution. Just think of it! If we died when we had stung others with sharp words, how many of us would be alive? And again, if we knew that we would die when we had stung, would we not curb our tongues to the benefit of ourselves and all others concerned.? This is surely an example that we may well take to heart and ponder repeatedly until we learn to snap our teeth together and keep our mouth closed whenever we are tempted to speak unkind words. If we can only do this, the time will come by and by when we shall cease to FEEL unkindly towards people, no matter what they do to us.

I can assure you in the case of Mrs. Heindel and myself, particularly since we came to Headquarters, that this chapter has been of more spiritual benefit to us than any other. It has helped us more than all the rest put together, though of course we are far, far from perfect yet. But what we have done, and what others have done with us here, is ample warrant for recommending this chapter to your earnest attention--coupled, perhaps, with the little story of the bees--for it will do as much for you if you read it and take it to heart one or twice a week.

AN INNER TRIBUNAL OF TRUTH

LAST week a visitor to Mt. Ecclesia told me that she had been studying all the different philosophies she could get hold of for about twenty years; also that she had in the past few years taken up the study of the Rosicrucian teachings, and that they appealed to her as being the absolute truth. She naturally expected me to give acquiescence to that sentiment, and was both amazed and dumbfounded when told that I did not so consider the teachings given me by the Elder Brothers and written in our various books.

To the Bushmen, the Kafirs, and other African savages who may develop a religious temperament, so far as they are capable of such a thing, it probably seems a great truth that there is a divine being of a higher nature than the human. From such men and from such a conception of religion there is gradual advance towards the transcendental philosophies which call out reverence in the most highly developed specimens of our human race. This gives us reason to believe that the evolution of man demands also an evolution of religion. We have climbed from the valleys of childlike ignorance to the point where we are today, and it would be absolutely contrary to the law of analogy to suppose that anything in the religious line which we have today is the ultimate; for if there is to be no more religious progress, there can be no more human progress either.

What, then, is the way to the heights of religious realization, and where may one find it? This seems to be the next logical question. The answer to it is that it is not found in books, either my own or anyone else's. Books are useful in so far as they give us food for thought on the subjects dealt with. We may or may not come to the same conclusions as the writer of the books, but so long as we take the ideas presented into our inner being and there work over them carefully and prayerfully, whatever comes out of the process is our own, nearer the truth than anything we can get from anyone else or in any other way.

The WITHIN then is the only worthy tribunal of truth. If we consistently and persistently take our problems before that tribunal, we shall in the course of time evolve such a superior sense of truth that, instinctively whenever we hear an idea advanced, we shall know whether it is sound and true or not. The Bible in a number of places exhorts us to beware of all kinds of doctrines floating about in the air because many are dangerous and unsettle the mind. Books are launched on the market which advance this, that, or the other system of philosophy. Unless we have established, or have started to establish, this inner tribunal of truth, we may be like the lady referred to above--wandering about from place to place, mentally speaking, all our lives and finding no rest, knowing little more at the end than in the beginning and perhaps even less.

Therefore my advice to the student would be never to accept or reject or follow blindly any authority, but to strive to establish the tribunal of truth within. Refer all matters to that tribunal, proving all things, and holding fast to that which is good.

EPIGENESIS AND THE LAW OF CAUSATION

SOME errors are so frequently expressed by students that they call for correction from time to time. The most general of these is the mistaken idea that everything which happens to us is the outcome or effect of some cause or action of our own in times past, generally in a past existence. Theoretically, students know that this attitude is wrong. They are aware that besides the destiny brought over with us from previous existences for liquidation in this life, we are every day exerting a causative influence by our acts. A considerable part of the deeds done in this body will work uot into effects before death terminates our stay in our present environment, while those deeds which are not thus liquidated will be held over and will form the foundation of the destiny of a future existence, where we may reap what we have sown. This destiny carried over from life to life is shown by our horoscope, and gives us certain characteristics and tendencies or lines of least resistance. It cannot be overlooked though that this destiny from the past gives us a certain bias or trend towards a particular line of action. But, nevertheless, there is comparative free will in a large percentage of our actions, leaving scope for the exercise of Epigenesis, the divine creative activity which is the basis of evolution.

As said, students all know this perfectly well, theoretically. But in dealing with problems of practical every-day life they seem to persistently take the attitude that all that that is, is an unfoldment of something that has already been. This is particularly true of students who have been studying the Eastern religions before taking up the Western Wisdom Teachings. By this mental attitude of ignoring Epigenesis they are retarding their soul growth to a greater extent than they are aware of. In fact something is happening to them similar to that which befalls the materialist during his post-mortem existence at the time when he lives on the Borderland between Purgatory and the First Heaven in a monotony most dreadful to contemplate. The Borderland is, so to speak, an eddy outside the stream of life where progress is at a standstill. The materialist is there because of his denial of post-mortem existence, which has put him out of touch with the spiritual currents that generate motion and action during that existence.

Similarly, when we constantly emphasize the Law of Causation and consistently and persistently ignore the Law of Epigenesis, we are placing ourselves outside the latter's line of action, and our opportunities for exercising its initiative are missed more often than not, with the result that we become more and more barren as the years go by. Whereas if we endeavor intelligently when considering the problems of life, exemplified in the actions of those about us as well as our own actions, to seek out the principle of Epigenesis and watch its operation, we shall find opportunities for initiative action opening up before us to an extent we have never before believed possible. By watching the way in which Epigenesis applies in other lives we shall learn how to apply it in our own.

I hope that you will keep this thought close to you and tha you may reap much benefit from a persistent practice of this principle.

THE PRESENT SORROW AND THE COMING PEACE

FROM the dim distant past there comes to us the voice of Isaiah in one of the grandest and most soul-inspiring of prophesies: "Unto us a child is born, unto us a son is given: and the government shall be upon his shoulder: and his name shall be called Wonderful, Counsellor, the mighty God, the everlasting Father, the Prince of Peace.

"Of the increase of his government and peace there shall be no end, upon the throne of David, and upon his kingdom, to order it, and to establish it with judgment and with justice from henceforth, even for ever." Nor is the song of the angel choir above the Galilean hills less potent to stir the soul with its sublime ideal: "On earth peace, and Good will toward men." But looking facts in the face as seen in the world today, such sayings seem little short of mockery; and from the customary viewpoint of the man in the street all the platitudes offered by the religionists cannot make the situation in the so-called, "Christian world" less odious.

But when we apply the cosmic scale of perspective and measurement, it is different. Goethe says well: "Who never ate his bread in sorrow, Who never spent the midnight hours Weeping, waiting for the morrow, He knows ye not ye heavenly powers." As with individuals, so with nations. Sorrow and suffering seem unfortunately to be the only teachers they will hear. Hence the necessity for their lessons. Viewing life as unending we are not dismayed at the so-called "loss of life" incident to the present war. Those killed will all be born again, and by their experience they will be better than they are now. Peace and good will are bound to come in time when we have learned to abhor war, hence we may well rejoice at the prospect and earnestly pray for its consummation. I would particularly urge students of the Rosicrucian Fellowship to unite in this prayer on Holy Night at midnight when the usual service is held in the Pro-Ecclesia by the workers on Mt. Ecclesia.

We enclose a little leaflet, "The Bible at a Glance," with seasonal greetings from the workers on Mt. Ecclesia, hoping that you may find the former both interesting and instructive.

GOD--THE SOURCE AND GOAL OF EXISTENCE

WE are again standing upon the threshold of a New Year, a time when it is a general custom to form one's aspirations into resolutions. As the students of the Rosicrucian teachings ought to be particularly interested in the matter of spiritual growth, I have thought that the following considerations may perhaps be of benefit at this time.

The word "holiness" has in the minds of many become associated with a long face and a hypocritical attitude of mind, so that people in the world are usually very shy of those who make professions of holiness. But that of course is not the true brand. The really holy man is not a kill-joy; he is not slothful in business; he does his duty fully, at home or in the shop, puts his heart into all his work; he is a worthy example of faithfulness, and is generally respected by all who know him, for his actions speak louder than words and command commendation. He is careful in his dealings with his fellow men, striving to owe no man anything but love, always ready and anxious to help others; he is in fact, a model man in all relations of life.

But this life of worldly rectitude is not itself a test of holiness. There are many splendid people in the world who live model lives for ethical reasons, and comport themselves in a manner that calls for the respect of all who know them. They are also charitable and are prominent, according to their station, in every good work. However, as said, this is not the test. The test showing the difference between the merely model man or woman and the holy one comes in the hours of leisure when the call of duty has been fulfilled for the time being. At that point it will be found that they ways of the worldly and the holy part, for at that time the worldly minded man turns to recreation, amusement, and pleasure for an outlet for his energy, or perhaps he pursues some favorite hobby according to the bent of his mind and as his means allow. It may be simple games or sports, or it may be song and music, theaters, parties, or any other means he can find to make time pass pleasantly.

But the holy man is as the steel touched with the lodestone and deflected by force from pointing to the pole. When once the heart has been touched by the lodestone of the love of God, duty may and does deflect it towards the affairs of the world which demand legitimate attention. The holy man not only does not shirk his worldly duty but he fulfills it better and more conscientiously than before giving himself to God. At he same time sub consciously he feels the yearning to return in mind to communion with the Father, which is analogous to the way the magnetized steel needle that has been deflected from the north exerts a pressure in the direction of the pole. The moment the call of duty has been fully answered and the pressure removed for the time being, the holy man's thoughts automatically turn towards the Divine. A ride in the street car to or from business is an opportunity for such meditation. The time spent in waiting for some one else is utilized in the same way. In short, never a moment of relaxation from worldly affairs comes to the holy man without his thoughts instantly turning to his source and goal--God.

We have heard of men who studied law while riding to and from business in street cars; others have learned languages by utilizing the spare moments which most people waste in idle, aimless, wandering thoughts. Let us learn a lesson from them, and during the coming year practice the habit of turning our thoughts to God during whatever scattered spare moments we have. If we practice this faithfully, we shall find ourselves greatly advanced upon the path of soul growth.

THE NECESSITY OF PUTTING TALENTS TO USE

THE Christ exhorted us to let our light shine, and in the parable of the talents He emphasized the points that TO WHOM MUCH IS GIVEN, OF HIM MUCH WILL BE REQUIRED, and that every one, no matter how little he has received, is expected to put it out to usury, to cast his bread upon the waters, so that it may return to him after many days and yield an increase. We are now standing near the beginning of another year. We have received the priceless Rosicrucian teachings. Hence it is required of us that we put his knowledge to some use in order to help those of our fellow men who have not yet received a solution of the problem of life and are seeking for light.

We are properly dislike conceited people who have an exaggerated idea of their own abilities and who bore other people to death with their undesired discourse. But the students of the Rosicrucian Fellowship seem to suffer from the opposite disease and temperament, which is just as bad. Self-depreciation, timidity, and mistrust of self squelch our ability and our talents, causing them to atrophy, just as do the eyes of animals which have left the sunlight and gone into caves to live, or as does the hand which is held inactive by the side for years and which loses its power to move. Our talents atrophy if not used. We shall be responsible for hoarding knowledge and withholding it from those who are seeking, just as much as the servant in the parable who buried his talent instead of working with it so that it might become greater.

We have always held that matters of belief should not be FORCED upon the attention of other people, but there are thousands of opportunities every year when we may say a word calculated to bring out an inquiry relative to our philosophy on the part of a friend addressed. It is perfectly legitimate to lead people on as long as they are interested. Paul exhorted his followers to be shod with a preparation of the Gospel, and if we follow that rule by preparing ourselves to answer questions intelligently, we shall find that people will be interested in what we have to say.

Just now people are intensely interested in life after death. But to answer their questions properly we must have enough of the Rosicrucian teachings by heart and we must have them at our fingers' ends. A little knowledge is dangerous in matters of religion and philosophy as well as in other things. You must have enough and of the right kind to make it worth while to enter the field of propaganda at all. But it is not difficult. While it may be very interesting and instructive to students of the Rosicrucian teachings who have become deeply interested in and have a good working knowledge of the philosophy to go into the mysteries of periods and evolutions, epochs and races, cosmic days and nights, et cetera, still all that is needed to help the man in the street is a thorough knowledge of the Laws of Consequence and Rebirth as they have been given in our literature. These are the vital principles which concern him most. They are the meat in the nut of the Rosicrucian teachings. If you can give them to a person who is in despair, either on account of having lost some one near and dear, or because the whole world seems upside down and he can find no place into which to fit, no way to get over the dead wall which confronts him, you may solve his problems for him in a logical and reasonable manner by showing how the law of Rebirth, coupled with the Law of Consequence, is constantly working for the good of humanity, and how he may gain whatever good he wants by working in harmony with these two great laws. You will thus have done him a signal service, and made considerable soul growth for yourself.

I would also suggest that classes be formed in the various study centers to study all that has been said in our literature concerning the workings of these two great laws, so that the students may fit themselves to render important service to the community by helping people to solve the problems of life which are so baffling to the great majority.

I trust that this suggestion may prove of benefit to you during the coming year.

THE NOBILITY OF ALL LABOR

A correspondent enthusiastic over the beauty, grandeur, and soul-satisfying nature of the Rosicrucian teachings bemoans the fate which has fettered her to a cook stove, a dishpan, the care of children, and the drudgery of housework; were she only free to take this new-found gospel, she would go into the wide world with the glad tidings for which she knows untold thousands are praying and seeking.

That would be well for our friend and those thousands, but what about the little children deprived of their mother's care? Do not forget the very important point that all who were hired to work in the Master's vineyard were standing idle in the market place. They had no hampering ties to hinder them from working there the whole day, and no one who is not free from former obligations may take up a life work of teaching others. If we aspire to that work by being faithful in the performance of our present duties, they way will open sometime and give us the legitimate call.

But about "drudgery"; the use of that word is all too common. The teacher talks of the drudgery of drumming the same lesson into the heads of children year after year; the mother talks of the drudgery of housework; the father complains of the drudgery of office or shop work; and so on down the line. Each thinks that if he or she were in the shoes of some one else, life would at once change to a grand, sweet song.

This is a fallacy. "Man that is born of woman is of few days and full of trouble." No matter where he is placed, there is only one method of relief, one way to overcome, and that is by adoption of the right attitude of mind.

A great gas engine going at full speed might defy an army of strong men to stop it, but a tiny speck of carbon deposited on the ignition point, or a small cam working loose, would quickly quell its energy. Thus a little soot, which we despise as dirt, can under certain circumstances accomplish more than many men. Therefore we should not extravagantly eulogize some as heroes and despise others as drudges. There are as noble souls mending stockings as ever graced presidential chairs. It all depends upon whether they put love into their work or not.

But what many really mean when they say "drudgery" is monotony. All work is routine more or less, and the constant performance of the same tasks often becomes monotonous. There is a very good reason why the present phase of our development includes this principle of routine. We are now getting ready for the fast approaching Aquarian Age with its great intellectual and spiritual development. This requires an awakening of the dormant vital body, whose keyword is REPETITION. The routine of our daily work furnishes this. If we rebel, it breeds monotony and retards progress. But if we leaven our labor with love, we shall advance ourselves greatly in evolution and reap the reward of contentment.

THE AQUARIAN AGE AND THE NEW COVENANT

AFTER writing the students' lesson and thinking over the various phases of Easter and the events happening around that time according to the Bible story, it occurred to me what a sealed book the Bible is to those who have not the Western Wisdom Teaching and a knowledge of esoteric astrology. So I decided to use this letter to elucidate one of the points that presented itself before my mind.

You probably remember that according to Luke (22nd chapter) the Christ sent Peter and John with instructions to look for a man bearing a pitcher of water and to enter into the house where he went, for there the passover was to be held. Later at that place, we are informed, He gave the apostles the bread and the water which constituted the New Covenant, declaring that he would no more drink the fruit of the vine. This is entirely misunderstood. To the great majority the man with the pitcher of water has no meaning, neither the fact that the passover was to be held at his house and not at some other place. Also people believe that Christ gave His disciples wine to drink, whereas the Bible says entirely the opposite. There is a great significance in this story when we read it as it is written and examine it in the light of the esoteric teaching.

First, let us remember how the leaders of humanity have given each new race a certain appropriate food, as elucidated thoroughly in the COSMO. Briefly, grain was given to Cain, the Second Race man, who was plant-like and had a vital body. To Abel, the Third Race man, who had a desire body, milk was supplied. To Nimrod, the Fourth Race man, who had a mind, meat was given. Wine was supplied by Noah to the Fifth Race man. It made him a Godless egotist, so that man's inhumanity to man has become a byword; but it also helped him to reach the nadir of his material evolution. Now, however, the spiritual evolution is about to begin, and altruistic ideas must be fostered, or at least started to germinating, so that they may be expressed by the Sixth Race. This again requires a change in diet.

While these steps in evolution have taken place, the sun by precision has circled the zodiac many times. But each step was inaugurated under a specific sign, and each was preceded and succeeded by minor cycles which were replicas of the great ages and evolutionary epochs. Thus the last six or seven thousand years while the sun went through Taurus, the sign of the Bull, Aries the sign of the Ram, and Pisces, the watery, fluidic sign have seen ages of material development, fostered by meat and wine. Even Christ at the beginning of His ministry turned water to wine, ratifying its continued use during the Piscean Age. But at the end of His earthly career He sent His disciples to prepare the passover in the house of the Water-bearer, and there abolished meat and wine by giving the bread and the water cup as the New Covenant for the Kingdom of God, where He is to reign as the Prince of Peace.

Could anything be plainer? Christ is the Sun Spirit, and when the sun passes over the equator at the vernal equinox in the sign of the Water-bearer, the Aquarian Age will be ushered in, in which the fleshless, non-alcoholic diet of the New Covenant will be in vogue and an era of altruism will dawn. We are beginning to feel this beneficent influence now, though it is still centuries away, and we are here to help prepare for that time. Therefore it behooves us to cleanse ourselves physically, morally, mentally, and spiritually that we may be a shining example to others and thereby lead them to the great Light which we have been fortunate enough to see. Let us also remember that the greater our knowledge, the greater also our responsibility for its right use, and unless we live up to these ideals, we shall merit the greater condemnation.

MEAT EATING AND FUR WEARING

A student who confesses that he is still addicted to flesh eating in some degree has occasionally an urge to speak to others on the Rosicrucian teachings, but always feels as if he were a hypocrite when he advocates vegetarianism. He asks us how he may overcome this habit and whether he should give up teaching others until he has himself attained.

This query has general interest, for though th students of the Rosicrucian teachings are sincere and earnest, they have the same imperfections as all other human beings or they would not be here; hence a letter on this subject may prove helpful to many.

It needs no argument to prove that you cannot effectively discourse on spirituality over a cocktail, nor advocate the harmless life while eating a steak. Furthermore, those who know your habits in daily life are always quick to notice the difference between what you preach and what you live. Therefore it is of course best to be able to live up to the teachings before commencing to convert others. At the same time it is too strong language to call any one a hypocrite because he advocates an ideal to which he has not yet attained. So long as one sincerely believes that the fleshless diet is right and tries to live accordingly, he is justified in advocating it even though occasionally he breaks the rule. The north star guides the mariner safely to his desired haven even though he never reaches the star itself. Similarly, if we set our ideals as high as the stars, we may not attain them in this life, but we shall always be the better for having them.

At the same time it would seem that with a little will power brought to bear it should not be very difficult for any one to abstain from tobacco, liquor, and flesh food. Surely the thought of the suffering that is caused the poor animals in the trains on their way to the slaughterhouse, and the agony which precedes the time when the blow is struck that ends their life or the time when the knife goes into their throat, ought to move any one who aspires to live the higher life and fill him with compassion for these poor dumb creatures which cannot defend themselves. For similar reasons the wearing of furs and feathers as ornaments should be dispensed with by the gentler sex among our ranks. It is equally inconsistent, and would doubtless cause adverse comments if any one should preach the gospel of harmlessness while thus arrayed.

Unfortunately the complexity of our civilization forces us to use leather for many things because no other material is available on the market to take its place; for example, for shoes, straps, etc. But nevertheless we ought to do all we possibly can to avoid making use of any material which comes from the body of an animal that requires its death. One of the blessings of this present war is that man is find out that meat is not an indispensable article of diet, and that we are far better off without alcohol. Let us hope that this is but the beginning of the end, and that man will soon cease to breed or hunt animals for their flesh and fur. Meanwhile let us all set the example and apply our will power to this end.

TOLERANCE OF OTHERS' BELIEFS

WE are here to live in the conditions as we find them and to learn the lesson provided by our environment. Those who are continually soaring in the clouds and seeking spiritual ideals to the neglect of their plain duties are just as mistaken in their efforts as those who wallow in the mire of material work, grubbing and grinding in their greed for the dollar. Both need help, but in opposite directions. One class needs to be pulled down till their feet are firmly planted upon earth; the other needs an uplift that they may see the light of heaven and begin to think of acquiring treasures there.

"One man's meat is another man's poison," and this applies to spiritual food at least equally as much as to physical. There is only one great truth--Diety--but it is many-sided. The angle of presentation which appeals to us may lack power to stir others; and, vice versa, their outlook upon truth may fail to meet our needs. Thus there is a reason for all the different religions in the world and the different views presented by the various cults and sects. Each has its mission to perform for the people among whom it is found, so we should be tolerant of all cults or religions even when those who profess them attack us and our views.

We should be satisfied to be known by our fruits, for that is the only true and valid test of individual religion. Does it make us better men and women, better fathers and mothers, sons and daughters, sisters and brothers, employers and employees? Does it make us better all-around citizens who may be looked up to in the community where we live? That is the test of true religion.

There is not so much danger of finding the materialist in our ranks, but unfortunately there is a tendency among people who espouse advanced teachings to soar in the clouds, forgetful of concrete conditions and earthly duties. This causes the average man and women to look askance at occultism and to regard those who study it as cranks, though their actions are no more the fault of occultism than it is the fault of good food when a weak stomach cannot digest it.

For this reason we should not only be tolerant of the beliefs of others and make it a rule never to belittle another faith, but we should watch ourselves to see that we LIVE the Rosicrucian teachings so as to do credit to them in our immediate environment.

THE PURPOSE OF WAR AND OUR ATTITUDE TOWARD IT

FROM time to time students in various parts of the world have been asking what should be their attitude toward the war and what purpose it serves from the spiritual standpoint. In answer we have pointed out in various articles the Rosicrucian teaching concerning the object of the war, namely, to turn the world towards God for consolation in its sorrow, and to rend the veil which exists between the visible and invisible worlds by helping a considerable number to acquire spiritual sight and the ability to communicate with those who have passed beyond. But though the explanations given have satisfied most occult students in a measure, there were others who did not feel satisfied therewith; they wanted something more directly bearing on the conditions. To them we pointed out the teaching in Lecture No. 13--"Angels as Factors in Evolution"--showing how human affairs are guided by the angels and archangels who act as family and Race Spirits, causing the rise and fall of nations as required for the evolution of the various groups of spirits under their guardianship.

As a final attempt to satisfy our students concerning this vital matter we send you herewith a lesson entitled, "The Philosophy of War," showing its application to the present conditions. We trust that this will give to all the needed explanation and help all to understand what is involved, so that they may render their hearty co-operation to end the struggle as soon as possible and secure the peace for which we all so ardently long.

But let us realize that there can be no peace worth having until militarism has received such a blow that it will not raise its head again for a long time. Many people hope that this will be the last war, and we ardently wish that we could believe it. People thought the same when Napoleon and his hordes overran Europe a hundred years ago, but time has proved that such hopes were vain. Peace is a matter of education, and impossible of achievement until we have learned to deal charitably, justly, and openly with one another, as nations as well as individuals. As long as we manufacture arms, peace will not become established. It should become our aim and object to do all we can toward the abolition of militarism in all countries and the establishment of the principle of arbitration of difficulties.

THE INNER POWER AND THE RESPONSIBILITY THAT GOES WITH IT

MANY years ago I spent a few weeks on a farm in Maine at the time when they were harvesting potatoes. As the wagons passed me, I noted that the potatoes were all large and of almost uniform size. So one day I congratulated the farmer on having such a fine crop of large potatoes. He walked over to a wagon and showed me that the bottom of the wagon was full of small potatoes. He also said that they had not been sorted in the field but that the jostling of the wagon over the rough road from the field to the barn brought the big potatoes to the top while the small ones sank to the bottom. "If you put the big ones at the bottom," he said, "they will rise to the top and the small ones will sink." And is this not just like life! People of representative appearance, of large qualities, rise to the top as we jostle one another over the rough places on the highway of life. "Yon cannot keep a good man down," is an old saying. He will rise to the top in spite of everything by virtue of the uplifting power within him. And similarly, no matter how often we put a small man on top, he will sink, because he lacks the inner power. We may build a house as large as we want and rear it above all other structures if we have material and labor in sufficient quantities, but the growth of man is from within, and no one can add a hairbreadth to the stature of another, physically, mentally, or morally. Each must work out his own salvation; he alone can determine whether he will remain in a lowly lot or rise to the top.

The farmer found that when his potatoes were carried over a smooth boulevard they remained mixed; but the rougher the road, the quicker the big potatoes rose to the top and the smaller ones sank to the bottom. In the great emergencies of life great opportunities await those who are ready to assume responsibilities and go to the front of the battle.

We are living in such a time, and if we aspire to rise, NOW is our greatest opportunity. The whole world is now asking for an answer to the riddle of life; inquiring whither the ship of humanity is sailing. And we have the answer. Upon us, therefore, rests the responsibility of living the teachings of the Elder Brothers and making them appeal to others by exemplary lives.

Many of our brothers are carrying the teachings of the Elder Brothers into the very trenches and enlightening those who are ready to be taught. Those of us who are still in our usual environment will find the interrogation point in many hitherto closed quarters. Let us therefore diligently seek the opportunities and improve them, for "unto whom much is given, of him shall much be required." I would suggest to the students that now is the time to see to it that the COSMO and our other literature, as far as possible, is in the libraries in their own cities; also that it is in a place where it is accessible and that it is being used. If a number of people inquire about it from time to time, though the Librarian may know nothing about it and perhaps even be hostile, the constant call for a certain book will finally force him to take notice. There is no doubt that the Fellowship teachings have within them an inner power that is bound to make a place for them in the world, but we shall acquire merit in proportion to the way in which we help to bring these teachings of the Elder Brothers to the notice of humanity in general. It is now vacation time and hence an especially propitious season for the dissemination of our soul-satisfying philosophy. Let us therefore all put forth an extra effort at this time. It will benefit others and ourselves also.

EQUIPOISE OF GREAT HELP IN TIMES OF STRESS

IN these days when our customs, habits, and business are being so radically interfered with by the great war no matter where on earth we live; when the flower of our manhood is being mowed down in millions by cannon; when even woman must leave her accustomed vocation as home maker to take part in the titanic struggle behind the fighting lines; when the weak, those who are either very old or very young, succumb to privation; how can one help being disturbed more or less according to one's individual suffering or one's proximity to the seething sea of hate and sorrow in what was once fair France or in the other battle-scarred sections? To remain undisturbed perhaps seems impossible. One cannot remain calloused in the face of such suffering. One student after describing the devastation of a shelled city, asks: "Can one help feeling very strongly about it?" No, Christ felt very strongly when He wept over the sins of Jerusalem, and He showed His righteous wrath when He drove the money changers out of the temple. But equipoise is undoubtedly one of the great lessons which we may learn from this war.

It is easy to be peaceful if one goes into the mountains and lives the life of a hermit. But what credit is it to keep our equipoise with no one to thwart, oppose, or vex us? It is more difficult, however, to keep a peaceful attitude in the industrial life of a city where relentless war is waged with the sword of competition and where existence is circumscribed by laws and custom. But it can be done, and it is being done by many who make no pretense to spirituality, but who have found that loss of balance interferes with their ambition. So they setout to train themselves in the practice of equipoise. It has been the invariable experience of such people that they have benefited greatly. Their health has improved, their happiness also, and their business efficiency has increased.

If such self-control can be attained by people in the world, and if so much benefit can accrue to them on that account under ordinary condition of life, those among us who aim at higher and nobler things and who have been endeavoring to follow the path for years ought to be examples of faith and hopefulness at this time, ought they not? We ought to be towers of strength to those who have not had the great enlightenment which it has been our privilege to obtain. And above all things, we ought to exert a constructive and upbuilding influence in this world crisis.

Therefore I have outlined in this month's lesson the secret causes which in the past have generated and fertilized the seeds that have now flowered into our present cataclysmic condition, and have indicated in a slight measure how we are now sowing the seeds of our future well or ill being; this in the hope that you will concentrate your thoughts constructively along the line indicated, and advocate in your sphere of life the views presented. Much sorrow may thus be averted in the future for thoughts are things, and if they are in harmony with the cosmic purpose to make all things work together for good, they will surely prosper.

THE OPTIMISTIC ATTITUDE AND FAITH IN ULTIMATE GOOD

SUPPOSE some one very close to you were undergoing a surgical operation. Naturally you would feel very much concerned, and your feelings would probably swing between fear and hope. Sometimes one emotion and sometimes the other would predominate. But consider what would be the effect upon the effect upon the patient if you were to voice your doubt and misgivings on every occasion. Fear always has a devitalizing and detrimental effect which makes it very difficult for the patient to recover, particularly as during the time of an illness he is less self-assertive and more negative than at times when he is in good, robust health. Thus while you were really anxious to help him and would do anything in your power to serve him, by that attitude of mind and the expression of such thoughts you would be really hindering him very much.

Something similar is taking place in the world at large at the present time. The human race is undergoing a necessary operation for spiritual cataract. The sorrow and suffering occasioned by the present war are doing much to tear the scale of materialism away from our eyes and rend the veil which divides us from those in the land of the living dead. The operation is painful in the extreme. Surely there is not a human being capable of humane feeling in the world who is not feeling in some measure for and with those who are actually engaged in the struggle. But if we are firmly convinced that "thoughts are things," it is our sacred duty to hold the most optimistic attitude of mind which it is possible for us to have at the present time.

I have no doubt that every student of the Rosicrucian Fellowship is doing all he can and giving all he can to alleviate the suffering and sorrow existing in the countries immediately affected, but it is the all-important mental attitude of optimism that is so difficult for many to cultivate and keep. Nevertheless it is our duty to do this, particularly in the light of our superior knowledge of the end in view, which will surely be attained. We cannot be glad that this thing is upon us, but we can be thankful that it is as certain to bring a great good to the world at large as it is that the sun rises every morning and sets at night.

We have an absolute faith in the wisdom and omnipotence of Deity. We know that it is a false accusation to say that "nature is red in tooth and claw," as some one has put it. Regardless of what it may seem to us with our limited vision, benevolence is the ruling factor in the world's evolution. Therefore each and every one of us should live up to the sacred obligation to always strive to hold an optimistic attitude and always emphasize our firm faith in the ultimate good which is to result from the present conditions. let us remember that when we are working with the trend of evolution it is like rowing a boat with the stream; our efforts will then have greater effect than if we take an attitude that is contrary to the world's good.

NOTE: THE LETTER FOR NOV. 1918 WAS DEVOTED TO BUSINESS MATTERS CONNECTED WITH OUR PUBLICATIONS, AND THEREFORE IS NOT INCLUDED HERE.

INCREASING THE LIFE OF THE ARCHETYPE

THIS is the last student's letter of the present year, and the thought at the ending of each cycle naturally turns to the fleetness of time and the evanescence of existence in the phenomenal world. It also reminds us of the preciousness of time and of our responsibility to use it to the best advantage for soul growth, "for what shall it profit a man if he shall gain the whole world, and lose his own soul?" Now is the seed time, and we are told that "unto whom much is given, of him shall much be required." Therefore we are accountable for what we have done or left undone to a greater measure than others who have not had the intimate knowledge of God's purpose which has been vouchsafed us through the Elder Brothers.

In this connection we should realize that every act of every human being has a direct effect on the archetype of his body. If the act is in harmony with the law of life and evolution, it strengthens the archetype and makes for a longer life in which the individual will get the maximum of experience and make soul growth commensurate with his status in life and capacity for learning. Thus fewer embodiments will be necessary to bring him to perfection than one who shirks the strain of life and endeavors to escape its burdens, or one who applies his forces destructively. In the latter type of life the archetype is strained and breaks early. Thus, those whose acts are contrary to the law shorten their lives and have to seek new embodiments a greater number of times than those who live in harmony with the law. This is another instance in which the Bible is correct when it exhorts us to do good that we may live long in the land.

This law applies to all without exception, but it has greater significance in the lives of those who are consciously working with the law of evolution than in those of others. The knowledge of these facts should add tenfold or a hundredfold to our zest and zeal for good. Even if we have started, as we say, "late in life," we may easily lay up more "treasure" in the last few years than in several previous lives. And above all, we are getting in line for an early start in lives to come.

Let us hope therefore that we have used to the best advantage the year which is now passing, and prepare to increase our efforts during the coming year.

THE LAW OF SUCCESS IN SPIRITUAL MATTERS

IT seems appropriate to commence our correspondence for 1919 by wishing you a happy and successful New Year. But the proverb says: "If wishes were horses, beggars would ride." Something more is required to secure success and happiness than mere wishes, and perhaps mine may bear better fruit if I explain to you the law of success.

The students of the Rosicrucian Fellowship are coversant with the fact that there is no "luck," and are quite well agreed with Mephisto in FAUST when he says: "Hoe closely luck is linked to merit, Does never to the fool occur. Had he the wise man's stone, I swear it, The stone had no philosopher.

But here a query will at once present itself to the minds of many: "Is it possible to reduce success to a law?" Yes, there is a law of success, as sure and immutable as any of the other great cosmic laws. And while I shall apply it only to spiritual matters, I cannot hide from you that it will also bring certain success in material affairs. But before you apply it in that direction, consider very carefully that to do so means spiritual suicide, for 'ye cannot serve God and Mammon." Rather, "seek ye first the kingdom of God, and His righteousness; and all these things shall be added unto you." I can testify to the truth of this promise, having lived by it for many years.

The law of success may then be stated as follows: First, determine definitely and clearly what you want--development of the healing power, extended vision, invisible helpership, the ability to lecture and carry the Rosicrucian message to others, etc.

Second, when you have set your goal, never harbor a thought of fear or failure for a moment, but cultivate an attitude of invincible determination to accomplish your object despite all obstacles. Constantly hold the thought, "I can and I will." Do not begin to make plans as to how to attain until you have reached the attitude of absolute confidence in yourself and in your ability to do what you desire, for a mind swayed by the slightest fear of failure cannot make plans that will fully succeed. Therefore be patient, and be sure first to cultivate absolute faith in yourself and your ability to succeed despite all odds.

When you have reached the point where you are fully persuaded that you can succeed and positively determined that you will succeed in some pursuit, there is no power on earth or in heaven that can withstand you in that particular pursuit; and you may then plan how to go about attaining your heart's desire with certainty of success.

I hope that you will apply this law earnestly in the pursuit of soul growth, not only during the coming year but in all future years.

www.ingramcontent.com/pod-product-compliance
Lightning Source LLC
Chambersburg PA
CBHW051546010526
44118CB00022B/2592